Teacher's Resource Book

Español para ti

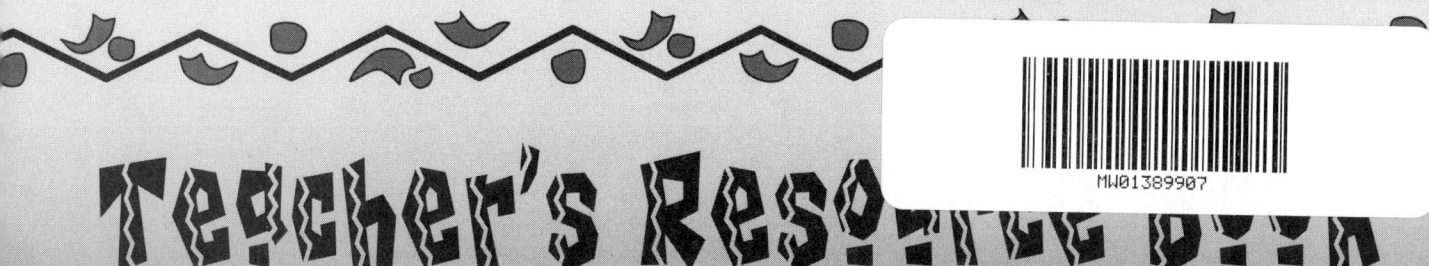

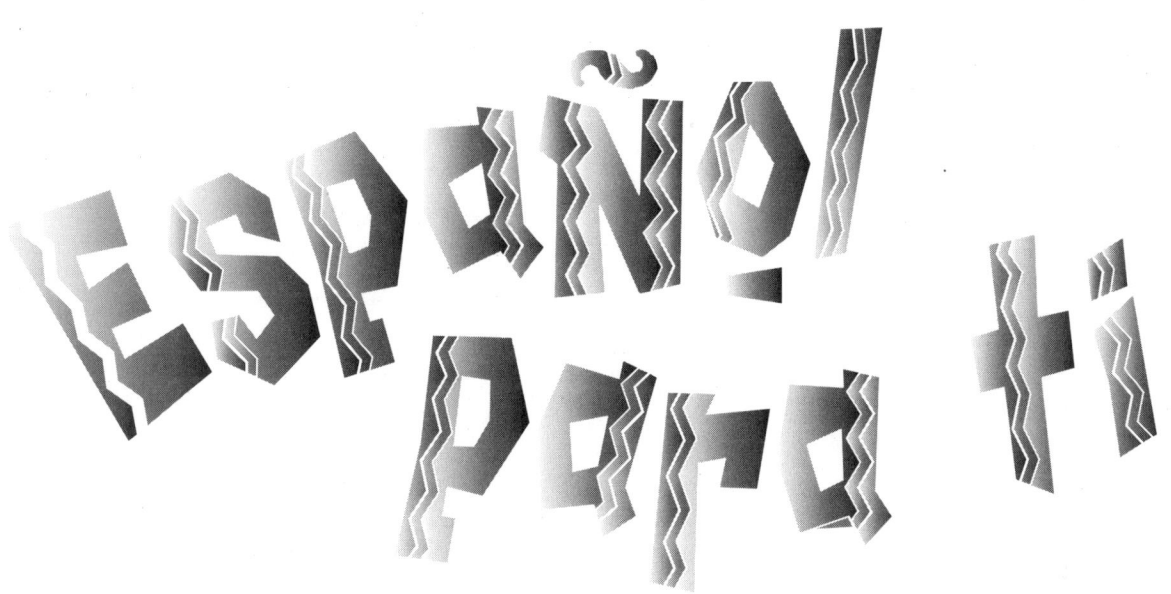

Elena Steele
K–12 Foreign Language Specialist
Clark County, Nevada, Public Schools

Holly Johnson
Español para ti Video Teacher

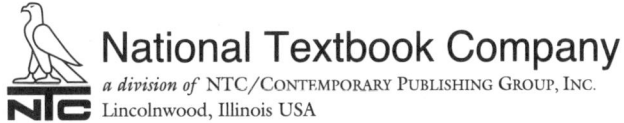

National Textbook Company
a division of NTC/Contemporary Publishing Group, Inc.
Lincolnwood, Illinois USA

Editorial and Production Management: Elm Street Publications, Wellesley, MA
Composition: Jan Ewing, Ewing Systems, New York, NY
Illustrations: Don Wilson, Len Shalansky

ISBN: 0-8442-0300-9

Published by National Textbook Company,
a division of NTC/Contemporary Publishing Group, Inc.
4255 West Touhy Avenue
Lincolnwood (Chicago), Illinois 60646-1975 U.S.A.
© 1998 NTC/Contemporary Publishing Group, Inc.

All rights reserved. No part of this book may be reproduced, stored in a retrieval system, or transmitted in any form or by any means, electronic, mechanical, photocopying, recording or otherwise, without the prior permission of the publisher.

Manufactured in the United States of America.

8 9 0 ML 0 9 8 7 6 5 4 3 2 1

ESPAÑOL PARA TI, Level Three

Table of Contents

Pattern for the Rosco Flag   1
Pattern for making the Rosco Flag, which can be reproduced on white or colored paper and glued to a stick or ruler.

Certificate for Course Completion   2
An optional certificate that can be duplicated for each child at the end of the year.

Family Letters   3
Four letters to send home, suggesting ways in which families can support their child's study of Spanish. Letters are appropriate to be sent home after the children finish Lesson 1, Lesson 20, Lesson 40, and Lesson 60.

Assessments   7
Midyear and End-of-year Assessments, with audio transcript and answer keys, plus a rubric for holistic assessment, which can be administered at various points during the year.
  Introduction to the Assessment Program   8
  Midyear Assessments   9
  End-of-year Assessments   30
  Rubric for Holistic Assessment   51

Number Cards   53
Large Number Cards for the numbers 1–20 and 10–100 (by tens).

Letter Cards   69
  Vowel Word Card   70
  Alphabet Chart   71
  Vowel Cards   72

Alphabet Cards   75

Blackline Masters   91
49 Blackline Masters that are needed for the Activity Lessons in the Teacher's Manual. Blackline Masters are numbered to correspond to the activity numbers in the Teacher's Manual and on the Activity Cassettes.

Teacher's Resource Book

1

Teacher's Resource Book

Family Letter 1

This letter can be used after the children have completed Lesson 1.

_____ (date)

Dear Parents,

Greetings! Or as they say in Spanish, **¡Hola!** (*Hello!*). If your child was in Spanish last year, welcome back! If you're new this year, we're glad to have you join us. Your child is going to be part of a new experience—watching videos while practicing Spanish along with classmates.

As our starting point this year, we are using what we learned in Levels 1 and 2. With **la maestra** (the on-screen video teacher), we'll review greetings, commands (e.g., run, walk, jump), and the numbers, as well as how to talk about the weather and various ways of expressing how one is feeling. We'll also sing familiar songs and learn new ones. We'll learn words for the various parts of the house, as well as items in the house such as furniture and appliances, and we'll expand our vocabulary for a favorite topic—food!

All our puppet friends—Rosco the wolf, Dora the cow, Ñico the toucan, and Jorge the giraffe—will share our experiences again and we'll root for them as they take part in the exciting game show **¡Repaso!** (*Review!*). One of the major areas of growth this year will be your child's ability to understand longer spoken passages and to say more complex expressions. By the end of the year, the children will even be able to read and write a little in Spanish and to sing the "*Alphabet Samba,*" a song about the Spanish alphabet.

Throughout the year, your interest and support are very important. Your praise, patience, and practice are crucial to your child's learning. Don't pressure your child to speak Spanish but do reward his or her attempts with ample praise. In the beginning, some children feel more comfortable singing in Spanish rather than speaking it. If this is the case with your child, let him or her teach you a song! Your child may enjoy being the teacher!

¡Adiós! (*Good-bye!*) is one of the expressions your child knows for saying good-bye to **la maestra** at the end of a video. So, until my next update to you on your child's progress in learning Spanish, let me bid you **¡Adiós!**

Sincerely,

_____

Teacher's Resource Book

FAMILY LETTER 2

This letter can be used after the children have completed Lesson 20.

_____ (date)

Dear Parents,

¡Hola! (*Hello!*) again. We've been very busy in Spanish. Part of the benefit of reviewing what we learned in Levels 1 and 2 has been seeing just how much we have accomplished over the last two years. We've been cementing that foundation by working on weather expressions; numbers 1 to 80; vocabulary for classroom objects, as well as for people and rooms in the school; parts of the body; colors; and clothing items. We've practiced words for the days of the week and seasons and categorized the months according to the season. In addition, we've reviewed saying the date, talking about our ages, and telling when our birthdays are. And we've "visited" a pool of dolphins with **la maestra** (the video teacher).

We've sung many songs from Levels 1 and 2 and have been learning a fun new counting song about elephants balancing on the thread of a spider's web! By playing games and doing activities with audiocassettes, we've been getting a lot of practice speaking Spanish. We've also been doing addition and subtraction problems, and we've been learning the vowels in Spanish.

The next several weeks will be an exciting time in Spanish class as we begin to learn the alphabet in Spanish with the help of a new friend **La Mano Mágica** (*The Magic Hand*). We'll also learn words for parts of the house—inside and outside—and take a "trip" with **la maestra** to shop for furniture. We'll learn how to answer the question **¿Por qué?** (*Why?*) in relation to how we feel, and we'll watch the puppets as they participate as contestants in the exciting television game show **¡Repaso!** (*Review!*).

We've much to look forward to in the coming weeks. Please continue to support your child's efforts to learn Spanish. Your interest is vital!

Sincerely,

_____

ESPAÑOL PARA TI, Level Three

Family Letter 3

This letter can be used after the children have completed Lesson 40.

_____ (date)

Dear Parents,

Your child has learned a lot of Spanish since our last letter. You should be very pleased! We have learned many words dealing with the house such as the words for parts of the house (e.g., roof, windows), for rooms in the house (e.g., living room, kitchen), and for furniture (e.g., sofa, lamp). We've also learned the importance of the home to people in Spanish-speaking countries, and we've heard the polite greeting **Mi casa es tu casa** (*My home is your home*). We've also reviewed the words for members of the family (e.g., mother, father, brother, sister, grandmother, grandfather), and we now know the entire Spanish alphabet and the numbers all the way to 100. We've sung many songs, and we've had fun watching **la maestra** (the video teacher) sing and dance to the *"Alphabet Samba."*

In the weeks to come we will be very busy! We will continue to learn house-related vocabulary, i.e., words for kitchen appliances (e.g., refrigerator, stove) and entertainment appliances (e.g., television, cassette player). We'll even "go shopping" for these appliances with **la maestra**. We'll learn to talk about activities we like to do in various seasons (e.g., play baseball, play football, ski, skate). We'll learn vocabulary for foods, and we'll gain an understanding of the cultural differences in mealtimes between our country and many Spanish-speaking countries.

You can help your child reinforce his or her growing ability to speak Spanish by providing opportunities to use it. If you are counting money or other items, ask your child to teach you to count it in Spanish. If you are talking about various family members, ask your child what that person would be called in Spanish. If you're talking about the colors of things like clothing or furniture, ask your child to teach you how to say the color in Spanish. If your child likes to sing, encourage him or her to teach you one of the songs he or she has learned in Spanish. You might even sing *"Are you Sleeping?"* and ask your child to sing a similar song he or she has learned in Spanish—***"Fray Felipe."***

We have learned a great deal and had a lot of fun in the process. We are looking forward to more fun with Spanish in the weeks ahead.

Sincerely,

_____

Teacher's Resource Book

Family Letter 4

This letter can be used after the children have completed Lesson 60.

_____ (date)

Dear Parents,

We have just finished a wonderful year of learning Spanish! Through the efforts of **la maestra** (the video teacher) and the puppets Rosco, Dora, Jorge, and Ñico, your child's ability to speak and understand the Spanish language has grown by leaps and bounds. There is almost no aspect of daily life that the children have not been exposed to in Spanish, including eating breakfast, lunch, and dinner; shopping; and playing. The children have even "participated" in a television game show!

Next fall the children will begin Level 4 of the Spanish program. You can prepare your child for the school year ahead by reviewing together what he or she already knows. Do this by taking advantage of opportunities to use and talk about Spanish. For example, at the start of the day, ask your child how he or she is and how one would say that in Spanish. When shopping for clothing or school supplies, remember that your child knows the Spanish names of many of these items, as well as how to express that she or he likes, wants, or needs these items. A trip to the grocery store or to a restaurant provides an opportunity to review words for different foods. If you and your child are participating in or talking about various activities (e.g., playing basketball, baseball, soccer, or football; skiing; skating; reading; jumping rope), ask your child how to say that he or she likes the activity. Ask your child to tell you in Spanish in what season he or she likes to play the sport.

A trip to the library is a chance to look through books on the various Spanish-speaking countries. Doing this together with your child would be a powerful statement that learning is important in itself and that you are interested in what your child is learning.

Above all, do not force your child to practice Spanish but rather take advantage of opportunities that naturally arise to give your child the chance to show what he or she knows.

It has been a true delight to watch your child's progress in Spanish. We are looking forward to another wonderful year ahead!

Sincerely,

_____

ESPAÑOL PARA TI, Level Three

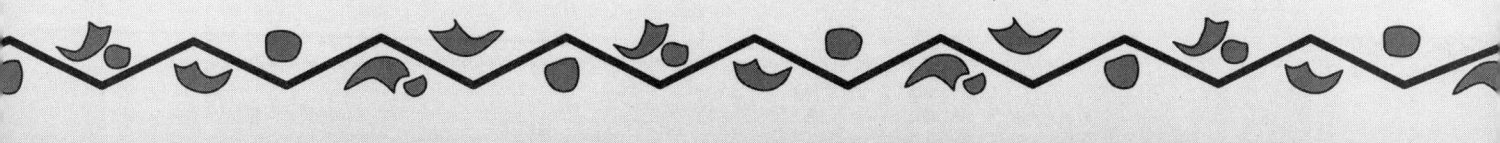

Assessments

INTRODUCTION TO THE ASSESSMENT PROGRAM

Welcome to the Assessment Program of Level 3 of *Español para ti*. The Assessment Program, which tests the major concepts taught in *Español para ti*, includes the following materials:
- Midyear Assessment (teacher's pages and pupil pages)
- End-of-year Assessment (teacher's pages and pupil pages)
- Rubric for holistic assessment

The Midyear Assessment is a set of assessment activities to be administered midway through Level 3, and the End-of-year Assessment is a set of assessment activities to be administered at the end of Level 3. To administer each set, you need the following materials:
- Assessment pages (provided in this Teacher's Resource Book)
- Assessment audio activities (located on Song Cassette, Side B)

The assessment pages for the midyear and end-of-year assessments provide (1) a teacher's page that describes each assessment activity and includes a suggestion for previewing each activity with the children, a transcript of what is said on the audiotape, and an answer key, and (2) a pupil page for each assessment activity on a blackline master. It is important to the assessment procedure that you feel comfortable administering the tests. For that reason we encourage you to keep in mind that YOU DO NOT NEED TO SPEAK OR READ SPANISH TO ADMINISTER OR CORRECT THESE TESTS.

Administering the assessments

Before doing the first assessment activity, we suggest you play a bit of the audiotape to establish that all children can hear what is being said. Provide each child with a copy of the pupil page for each activity and a pencil or crayon. Before playing each activity on the Song Cassette, make sure children have the corresponding pupil page in front of them and preview the activity by using the description provided on the following pages. (You may decide to hand out each pupil page just prior to playing the activity on the audiotape so that the children are not distracted by looking at other pages.)

Next, play the activity on the audiotape (Song Cassette, Side B). Note that the audio transcription of each activity includes English translations for any Spanish spoken on the tape. The children will hear each cue three times. The first time they should listen, the second time they should mark their answer, and the third time they should check their answer.

After the children have completed each activity, you may wish to give them a short break before they move on to the next activity. For your convenience in correcting the assessments, the answers are provided in the margin in a miniature reproduction of the pupil page next to the description of each activity.

MIDYEAR ASSESSMENT OVERVIEW

The Midyear Assessment covers the following topics:
    Pupil page 1:   Classroom items
    Pupil page 2:   Numbers 1–90
    Pupil page 3:   Commands
    Pupil page 4:   Seasons and weather
    Pupil page 5:   Clothing and colors
    Pupil page 6:   School places and people
    Pupil page 7:   Dates
    Pupil page 8:   Parts of the body
    Pupil page 9:   Geometric shapes and vowels
    Pupil page 10: Animals and feeling expressions

Materials to gather:

To administer the Midyear Assessment you will need:

- A cassette player
- Song Cassette, Side B
- Midyear Assessment pupil pages 1–10, one of each page per child
- One pencil or crayon per child
- For Midyear Assessment pupil page 5: crayons in black, blue, brown, gray, green, orange, pink, purple, red, white, and yellow for each child

Use the Introduction to the Assessment Program on page 8 and the following pages to guide you in administering the Midyear Assessment.

Teacher's Resource Book

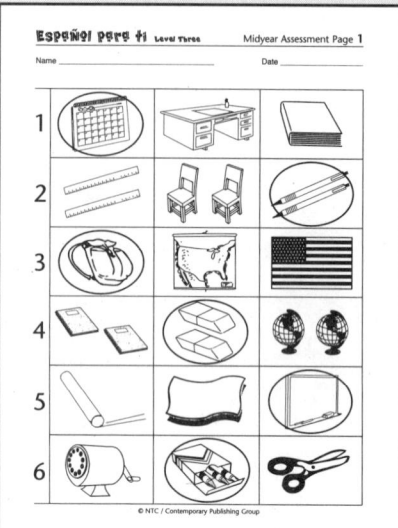

Midyear Assessment
Page 1 Answer Key

MIDYEAR ASSESSMENT PAGE 1

Classroom items

Make sure the children have Midyear Assessment pupil page 1 in front of them. Point out that the pictures in each row show things found in a classroom. Check to be sure all children recognize the objects pictured. For each row, doña Elena is going to name an object or objects. Children should circle the picture named. Doña Elena will say each cue three times. The first time, they should listen. The second time, they should circle their answer. The third time, they should check over their answer.

Before starting the assessment, check to be sure everyone can hear the tape. Then play the audiotape, turning it off at the end of assessment activity 1. You may wish to take a short break before moving on to the next assessment activity.

Audio transcription:

¡Hola, clase! (*Hello, class!*) Let's find out how much Spanish you have learned. You have a page that shows pictures of various objects found in a classroom. Listen carefully and circle the object or objects that I name. Let's look at row 1. Listen first, then circle, then check over your answer.

> Row 1. **El calendario. El calendario. El calendario.** (*calendar*) **Muy bien.** (*Very good.*)
>
> Next, go to row 2. **Los lápices. Los lápices. Los lápices.** (*pencils*)
>
> Now, let's go to row 3. **La mochila. La mochila. La mochila.** (*book bag, backpack*)
>
> Ready for row 4? Okay. **Las gomas. Las gomas. Las gomas.** (*erasers*)
>
> Here's row 5. **La pizarra. La pizarra. La pizarra.** (*chalkboard*)
>
> Just one more. Row 6. **Los colores. Los colores. Los colores.** (*crayons*)

Excelente, clase. (*Excellent, class.*)

MIDYEAR ASSESSMENT PAGE 2

Numbers 1–90

Make sure the children have Midyear Assessment pupil page 2 in front of them. Point out the eight numbered spaces on the page. For items 1 through 4, doña Elena is going to say a number from 1 to 90 followed by the question ¿Y uno más? (*And one more?*). Children are to write the number that is 1 more than the number doña Elena stated. For items 5 through 8, the children are to write down the math problem doña Elena says but not solve it until she has finished. Now play the audiotape, turning if off at the end of assessment activity 2. Have the children solve the problems after you turn off the tape.

Audio transcription:

Now let's go to page 2 and have some fun with numbers. For each of the first items on your paper, I am going to say a number. You are to write down the number that is **uno más** (*one more*) than the number I said. Are you ready? Let's begin.

> Item 1. **Uno. Uno. Uno.** (*one*) ¿Y uno más? (*And one more?*)
>
> Was that an easy one? Here's the next one. Item 2. **Veinticuatro. Veinticuatro. Veinticuatro.** (*twenty-four*) ¿Y uno más? (*And one more?*)
>
> Let's try another one. Item 3. **Cincuenta y tres. Cincuenta y tres. Cincuenta y tres.** (*fifty-three*) ¿Y uno más? (*And one more?*)
>
> And here's our last one in this section. Item 4. **Ochenta y siete. Ochenta y siete. Ochenta y siete.** (*eighty-seven*) ¿Y uno más? (*And one more?*)

Now let's work on items 5 through 8. For each item, I'm going to say a math problem. Do you remember that **más** means *more* or *plus* and **menos** means *less* or *minus*? Listen carefully and write down each problem. Don't try to solve the problem yet. You will have time to do that after you've written down all 4 problems. Here we go. Listen carefully. I'll say each problem three times.

> Item 5. **Diez más tres son ... . Diez más tres son ... . Diez más tres son ... .** (*ten plus three are . . .*) Have you finished writing the problem?
>
> Here's item 6. **Treinta menos cinco son ... . Treinta menos cinco son ... . Treinta menos cinco son ... .** (*thirty minus five are . . .*)
>
> Let's try another one. Here's item 7. **Sesenta y dos más quince son ... . Sesenta y dos más quince son ... . Sesenta y dos más quince son ... .** (*sixty-two plus fifteen are . . .*)
>
> And here's the final problem. **Cincuenta y cuatro menos once son ... . Cincuenta y cuatro menos once son ... . Cincuenta y cuatro menos once son ... .** (*fifty-four minus eleven are . . .*)

Now solve the problems you have written down.

Midyear Assessment
Page 2 Answer Key

Midyear Assessment
Page 3 Answer Key

Midyear Assessment Page 3

Commands

Make sure the children have Midyear Assessment pupil page 3 in front of them. Point out that there are three pictures of Antonio in each row. Doña Elena is going to tell Antonio to do something. Children should circle the picture that shows Antonio doing what doña Elena told him to do. Doña Elena will say each command three times. You may wish to remind the children that Antonio is called by several different nicknames (including Toño). Now play the audiotape, turning it off at the end of assessment activity 3.

Audio transcription:

Let's go to page 3. You see four rows of pictures of our friend Antonio. For each row of pictures, I'm going to tell Antonio to do something. You circle the picture that shows Antonio doing what I told him. You will hear each command three times.

Are you looking at the pictures in row 1? **Bien.** (*Good.*) **Antonio, ¡dame las flores! ¡Dame las flores! ¡Dame las flores!** (*Give me the flowers!*)

Now look at row 2. **Antonio, ¡dibuja un elefante! ¡Dibuja un elefante! ¡Dibuja un elefante!** (*Draw an elephant!*)

Look at row 3. **¿Listos?** (*Ready?*) **Toño, ¡salta! ¡Salta! ¡Salta!** (*Jump!*)

Here's the last one. Row 4. **Toño, ¡borra el elefante! ¡Borra el elefante! ¡Borra el elefante!** (*Erase the elephant!*)

Fantástico, niños. (*Fantastic, children.*)

ESPAÑOL PARA TI, Level Three

Midyear Assessment Page 4

Seasons and weather

Make sure the children have Midyear Assessment pupil page 4 in front of them. Point out that in each row there are four pictures. Doña Elena is going to name a season and typical weather for that time of year. She will say each season and its weather three times. For each of her statements, children should circle the season and the weather she mentions. Be sure they understand that in each row of pictures they must make <u>two</u> circles. Now play the audiotape, turning it off at the end of assessment activity 4.

Audio transcription:

Now let's go to page 4. What do we have here?—seasons and weather. Circle the season and the weather that I tell you. I will say each season and weather three times.

I'm ready for number 1. Let's go. **En la primavera llueve. En la primavera llueve. En la primavera llueve.** (*In the spring it rains.*)

Here's number 2. **Hace viento en el otoño. Hace viento en el otoño. Hace viento en el otoño.** (*It's windy in the fall.*)

How are you doing? Let's try number 3. **En el invierno nieva. En el invierno nieva. En el invierno nieva.** (*In winter it snows.*)

Here's the last one. **Hace calor en el verano. Hace calor en el verano. Hace calor en el verano.** (*In summer it's hot.*)

Muy bien, clase. (*Very good, class.*)

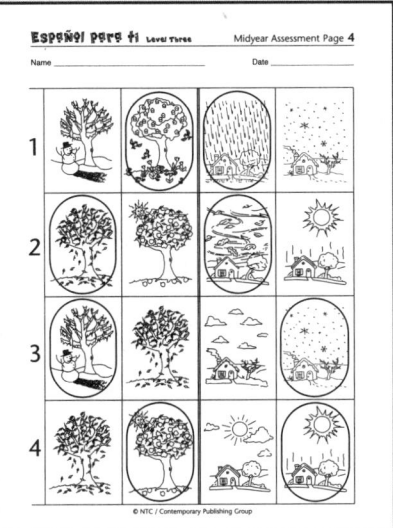

Midyear Assessment
Page 4 Answer Key

Teacher's Resource Book

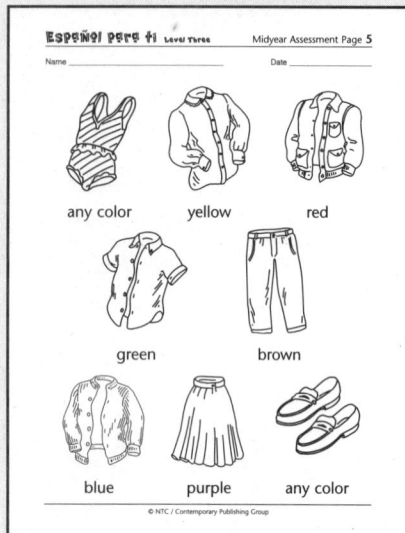

Midyear Assessment
Page 5 Answer Key

MIDYEAR ASSESSMENT PAGE 5

Clothing and colors

Additional materials: crayons in black, blue, brown, gray, green, orange, pink, purple, red, white, and yellow, one of each color per child.

Make sure children have Midyear Assessment pupil page 5 in front of them. Point out that on the page are pictures of clothing. If necessary, identify each item of clothing in English. Doña Elena is going to instruct the children to color each piece of clothing. They have to color only a small amount of each clothing piece when it is named. They will have time to finish coloring at the end of the activity. Now play the audiotape, turning it off at the end of assessment activity 5. Remember to allow children time to finish coloring after you turn off the tape.

Audio transcription:

Now let's go to page 5 and give the pieces of clothing some color! Are you ready to color? Remember to listen for the item of clothing and the color you should make it. You will hear each instruction three times.

Colorea la chaqueta rojo. Colorea la chaqueta rojo. Colorea la chaqueta rojo. (*Color the jacket red.*)

Here's the next one. **Colorea el suéter azul. Colorea el suéter azul. Colorea el suéter azul.** (*Color the sweater blue.*)

Listen again. **Colorea los pantalones café. Colorea los pantalones café. Colorea los pantalones café.** (*Color the pants brown.*)

What color shall we make **la blusa**? **Colorea la blusa amarillo. Colorea la blusa amarillo. Colorea la blusa amarillo.** (*Color the blouse yellow.*)

There are only a few pieces of clothing left. **Colorea la falda morado. Colorea la falda morado. Colorea la falda morado.** (*Color the skirt purple.*)

What's left? **Colorea la camisa verde. Colorea la camisa verde. Colorea la camisa verde.** (*Color the shirt green.*)

¡**Perfecto, niños!** (*Perfect, children!*) Now finish coloring in the pictures and color **los zapatos** (*shoes*) and **el traje de baño** (*bathing suit*) whatever color you want.

ESPAÑOL PARA TI, Level Three

Midyear Assessment Page 6

School places and people

Make sure children have Midyear Assessment pupil page 6 in front of them. Point out that down the left side of the page are pictures of various people and down the right side are pictures of places in the school. Doña Elena is going to tell them where each person is. Children should draw a line from the person to the place doña Elena says the person is. She will say each statement three times. Now play the audiotape, turning it off at the end of assessment activity 6.

Audio transcription:

Now turn to page 6. I'm going to tell you where each person is. You will hear each statement three times. Draw a line from the person to the place. ¿**Listos?** (*Ready?*) Here we go.

El secretario está en la cafetería. El secretario está en la cafetería. El secretario está en la cafetería. (*The secretary is in the cafeteria.*)

¿**Dónde está la maestra?** (*Where is the female teacher?*) **La maestra está en la oficina. La maestra está en la oficina. La maestra está en la oficina.** (*The female teacher is in the office.*)

Ready for the next one? **El maestro está en la biblioteca. El maestro está en la biblioteca. El maestro está en la biblioteca.** (*The male teacher is in the library.*)

Last one. **El enfermero está en el patio. El enfermero está en el patio. El enfermero está en el patio.** (*The nurse is on the playground.*)

Now we know where everyone is. ¡**Excelente, clase!** (*Excellent, class!*)

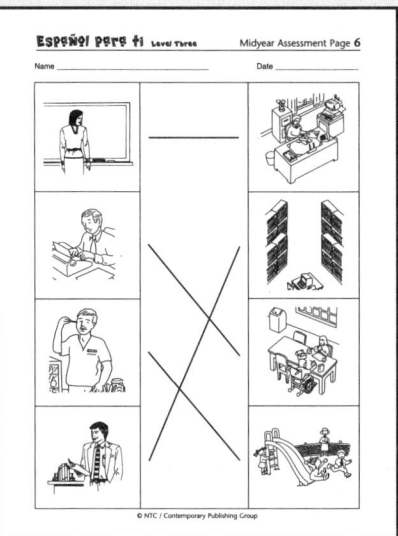

Midyear Assessment
Page 6 Answer Key

Teacher's Resource Book

Midyear Assessment
Page 7 Answer Key

MIDYEAR ASSESSMENT PAGE 7

Dates

Make sure the children have Midyear Assessment pupil page 7 in front of them. Point out that there are four dates in each row. Each square shows a picture for the month and a date in that month. Doña Elena is going to ask Rosco and Dora to name a date. Children should circle the date that they hear. Doña Elena will ask the question three times and the puppets will answer. Now play the audiotape, turning it off at the end of assessment activity 7.

Audio transcription:

Let's go to page 7. You see some dates. In this activity our two ¡Repaso! (Review!) rivals are with us. I'm going to ask Rosco and Dora what date it is. Listen as they say each date. Then circle the date on your paper. You will hear the questions and answers three times.

Are you looking at the dates in row 1? **Bien.** (Good.)
Rosco, ¿cuál es la fecha? El seis de junio.
Rosco, ¿cuál es la fecha? El seis de junio.
Rosco, ¿cuál es la fecha? El seis de junio.
(Rosco, what is the date?)   (June 6)

Ready for row 2?
Dora, ¿cuál es la fecha? El veintiuno de enero.
Dora, ¿cuál es la fecha? El veintiuno de enero.
Dora, ¿cuál es la fecha? El veintiuno de enero.
(Dora, what is the date?)   (January 21)

Now look at row 3.
Rosco, ¿cuál es la fecha? El trece de septiembre.
Rosco, ¿cuál es la fecha? El trece de septiembre.
Rosco, ¿cuál es la fecha? El trece de septiembre.
(Rosco, what is the date?)   (September 13)

Now, let's see what Dora has to say this time.
Dora, ¿cuál es la fecha? El quince de noviembre.
Dora, ¿cuál es la fecha? El quince de noviembre.
Dora, ¿cuál es la fecha? El quince de noviembre.
(Dora, what is the date?)   (November 15)

¡Fabuloso, clase! (Fabulous, class!)

ESPAÑOL PARA TI, Level Three

MIDYEAR ASSESSMENT PAGE 8

Parts of the body

Make sure children have Midyear Assessment pupil page 8 in front of them. Point out the lines that appear at various parts of the body of *Mr. Bones* (**El señor Huesos**). Doña Elena is going to say a number followed by a part of the body. Children should locate the part of the body and write the number on the line that appears next to the body part. Remind them that doña Elena will say each number and body part three times. Now play the audiotape, turning it off at the end of assessment activity 8.

Audio transcription:

Ready for activity 8? Are you looking at the picture of **El señor Huesos** (*Mr. Bones*)? I'm going to say a number and a part of the body. Locate the body part and write its number on the line provided. I will say the name of each body part three times. Here we go. Listen carefully.

Number 1, **los ojos.** Number 1, **los ojos.** Number 1, **los ojos.** (*eyes*)

Number 2, **el brazo.** Number 2, **el brazo.** Number 2, **el brazo.** (*arm*)

Let's try another. Number 3, **la mano.** Number 3, **la mano.** Number 3, **la mano.** (*hand*)

Number 4, **las piernas.** Number 4, **las piernas.** Number 4, **las piernas.** (*legs*)

Number 5, **el dedo.** Number 5, **el dedo.** Number 5, **el dedo.** (*finger*)

Ready for another? Number 6, **los pies.** Number 6, **los pies.** Number 6, **los pies.** (*feet*)

Here's the last one. Number 7, **la boca.** Number 7, **la boca.** Number 7, **la boca.** (*mouth*)

Muy bien, clase. ¡Excelente! (*Very good, class. Excellent!*) You are remembering so much!

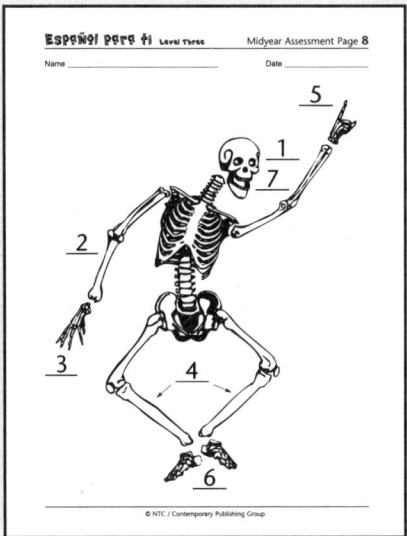

Midyear Assessment
Page 8 Answer Key

Teacher's Resource Book

MIDYEAR ASSESSMENT PAGE 9

Geometric shapes and vowels

Make sure the children have Midyear Assessment pupil page 9 in front of them. Point out that the page is divided into two sections. In the first section, doña Elena is going to say the name of a geometric shape. The children should draw each shape. In the second part, they are going to hear the seven days of the week and fill in the missing vowel in each word. Now play the audiotape, turning it off at the end of assessment activity 9.

Audio transcription:

Do you have page 9 in front of you? On the top part of the paper, you are going to draw the geometric shape I say next to the appropriate number. I will name each shape three times. Are you ready?

Number 1. **Dibuja un triángulo. Dibuja un triángulo. Dibuja un triángulo.** (*Draw a triangle.*)

Number 2. **Dibuja un cuadro. Dibuja un cuadro. Dibuja un cuadro.** (*Draw a square.*)

Number 3. **Dibuja un círculo. Dibuja un círculo. Dibuja un círculo.** (*Draw a circle.*)

It's fun to spell words and you've been learning the vowels in Spanish: **a, e, i, o, u.** Now look at the bottom part of your page. Listen carefully as I say each day of the week and fill in the missing vowel in each word. I will say each day three times. Ready? Let's go.

Number 1, **lunes. Lunes. Lunes.** (*Monday*)

Number 2, **martes. Martes. Martes.** (*Tuesday*)

Here comes the next one. Number 3, **miércoles. Miércoles. Miércoles.** (*Wednesday*)

Number 4, **jueves. Jueves. Jueves.** (*Thursday*)

Ready for Number 5? **Bien.** (*Good.*) Number 5, **viernes. Viernes. Viernes.** (*Friday*)

Number 6, **sábado. Sábado. Sábado.** (*Saturday*)

And one last day of the week. Number 7, **domingo. Domingo. Domingo.** (*Sunday*)

¡Perfecto, niños! (*Perfect, children!*)

Midyear Assessment Page 9 Answer Key

1. △
2. □
3. ○

1. l u nes
2. m a rtes
3. miérc o les
4. juev e s
5. viern e s
6. sábad o
7. dom i ngo

ESPAÑOL PARA TI, Level Three

MIDYEAR ASSESSMENT PAGE 10

Animals and feeling expressions

Make sure the children have Midyear Assessment pupil page 10 in front of them. Point out that on the paper are four rows of pictures of animals and that each animal is expressing a feeling. For each row, doña Elena is going to say what one of the animals is saying. Children should circle the picture that matches what doña Elena has said. Now play the audiotape, turning it off at the end of assessment activity 10.

Audio transcription:

Let's look at page 10. For each row, I'm going to tell you what one of the animals is saying. Circle the picture that matches what I say. I will tell you three times what each animal is saying. Are you ready?

Row 1. **Tengo hambre. Tengo hambre. Tengo hambre.** (*I'm hungry.*)

Let's try row 2. **Tengo frío. Tengo frío. Tengo frío.** (*I'm cold.*)

Row 3. **Tengo sueño. Tengo sueño. Tengo sueño.** (*I'm sleepy.*)

And here's the last one. Row 4. **Tengo dolor. Tengo dolor. Tengo dolor.** (*I'm hurt.*)

¡**Qué bueno, clase!** (*What a good job, class!*) We're finished.

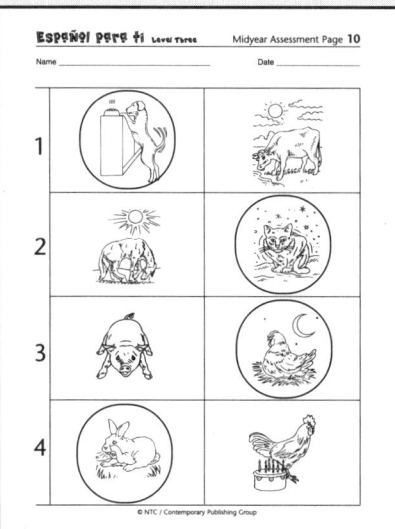

Midyear Assessment
Page 10 Answer Key

Teacher's Resource Book

Español para ti Level Three

Midyear Assessment Page **1**

Name _____ Date _____

Español para ti Level Three   Midyear Assessment Page **2**

Name _____   Date _____

1. _____   5.

2. _____   6.

3. _____   7.

4. _____   8.

Español para ti Level Three — Midyear Assessment Page 3

Name _____   Date _____

1
2
3
4

© NTC / Contemporary Publishing Group

Español para ti Level Three   Midyear Assessment Page **4**

Name _____ Date _____

Español para ti Level Three — Midyear Assessment Page 5

Name _____ Date _____

Español para ti Level Three   Midyear Assessment Page 6

Name _____   Date _____

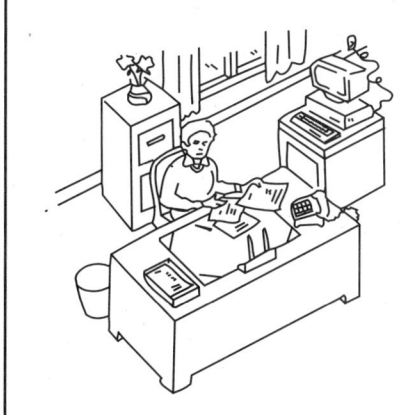

© NTC / Contemporary Publishing Group

Español para ti Level Three Midyear Assessment Page 7

Name _____ Date _____

1	7	16	6	20
2	2	21	1	20
3	13	23	31	3
4	25	9	5	15

© NTC / Contemporary Publishing Group

Español para ti Level Three

Midyear Assessment Page **8**

Name _____ Date _____

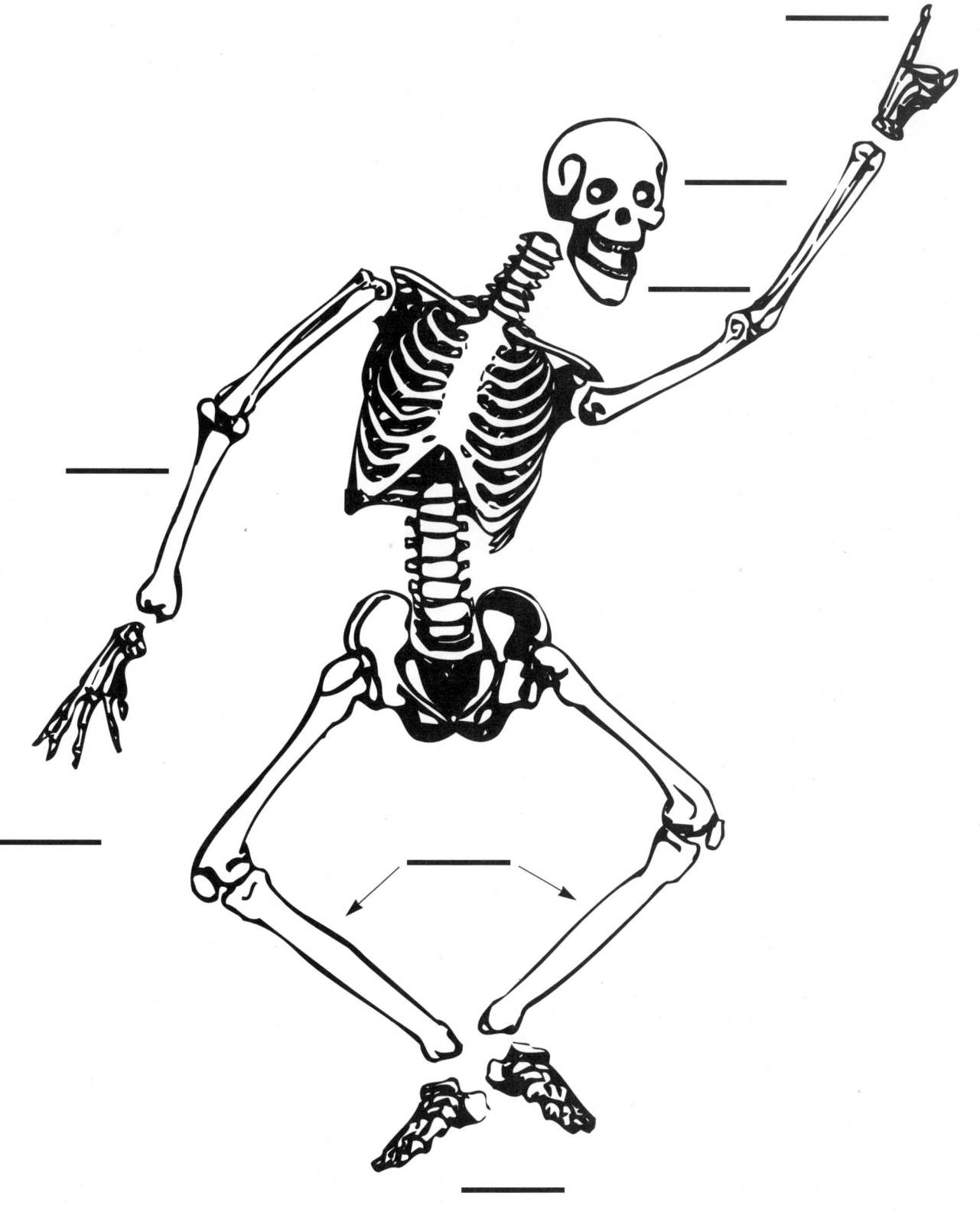

Name _____   Date _____

1.

2.

3.

---

1. l__nes

2. m__rtes

3. miérc__les

4. juev__s

5. viern__s

6. sábad__

7. dom__ngo

Español para ti Level Three

Midyear Assessment Page **10**

Name _____   Date _____

1		
2		
3		
4		

© NTC / Contemporary Publishing Group

END-OF-YEAR ASSESSMENT OVERVIEW

The End-of-year Assessment covers the following topics:
- Pupil page 1: Parts of the house
- Pupil page 2: Family members and rooms of the house
- Pupil page 3: The alphabet
- Pupil page 4: Furniture
- Pupil page 5: Kitchen appliances
- Pupil page 6: Big numbers and entertainment appliances
- Pupil page 7: Seasonal activities
- Pupil page 8: (**No**) **Me gusta** (*I [don't] like*), fruits, and writing
- Pupil page 9: Mealtimes and foods
- Pupil page 10: Identifying various questions

Materials to gather

To administer the End-of-year Assessment you will need:
- A cassette player
- Song Cassette, Side B
- End-of-year Assessment pupil pages 1–10, one of each page per child
- A pencil or crayon for each child

Use the Introduction to the Assessment Program on page 8 and the following pages to guide you in administering the End-of-year Assessment.

END-OF-YEAR ASSESSMENT PAGE 1

Parts of the house

Make sure children have End-of-year Assessment pupil page 1 in front of them. Point out that on the left side of the page are the numbers 1 to 6 and that on the right side of the page are pictures of parts of the house. For each number, doña Elena is going to say a part of the house. Children are to draw a line from each number to its corresponding house part. Doña Elena will say each cue three times. The first time, the children should listen. The second time, they should draw a line for their answer. The third time, they should check over their answer.

Before starting the assessment, you may wish to check if everyone can hear the tape. Then play the audiotape, turning it off at the end of assessment activity 1. You may wish to take a short break before moving on to the next assessment activity.

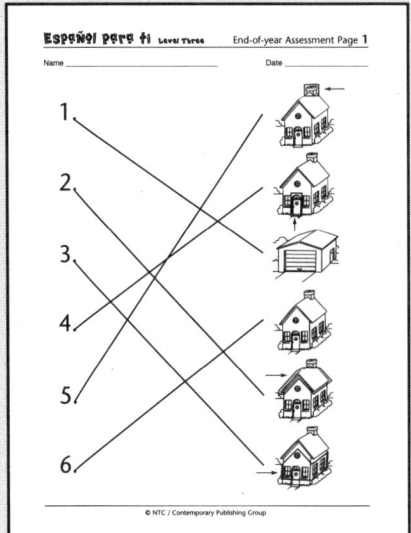

End-of-year Assessment
Page 1 Answer Key

Audio transcription:

Niños, ¿están listos? (*Children, are you ready?*) I'm going to say a number from 1 to 6 followed by the word for a part of the house. You will draw a line from the number to the drawing of the part of the house. I will say each item three times.

Number 1, **el garaje. El garaje. El garaje.** (*garage*)

Was that an easy one? Try this one. Number 2, **el techo. El techo. El techo.** (*roof*)

Number 3, **las ventanas. Las ventanas. Las ventanas.** (*windows*)

Here's number 4. **La puerta. La puerta. La puerta.** (*door*)

Number 5, **la chimenea. La chimenea. La chimenea.** (*chimney*)

And one more. Number 6, **la casa. La casa. La casa.** (*house*)

¡Fantástico, niños! (*Fantastic, children!*)

Teacher's Resource Book

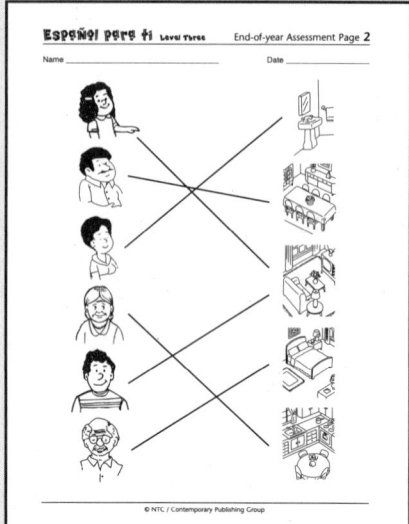

End-of-year Assessment
Page 2 Answer Key

END-OF-YEAR ASSESSMENT PAGE 2

Family members and rooms of the house

Make sure the children have End-of-year Assessment pupil page 2 in front of them. Point out that on the left side of the page are pictures of family members. On the right side of the page are pictures of rooms in the house. Doña Elena is going to say where each family member is. Children are to draw a line from the family member to the appropriate room. Now play the audiotape, turning it off at the end of assessment activity 2.

Audio transcription:

Now let's go to page 2. ¿Dónde está la familia? (*Where is the family?*) I'm going to tell you where each family member is. Draw a line from the family member to the room the person is in. I will say each item three times. Ready?

La mamá está en el baño. La mamá está en el baño. La mamá está en el baño. (*The mother is in the bathroom.*)

Try another one. **El hijo está en la sala. El hijo está en la sala. El hijo está en la sala.** (*The son is in the living room.*)

La abuela está en la cocina. La abuela está en la cocina. La abuela está en la cocina. (*The grandmother is in the kitchen.*)

Ready for the next one? Here it is. **El papá está en el comedor. El papá está en el comedor. El papá está en el comedor.** (*The father is in the dining room.*)

El abuelo está en el cuarto. El abuelo está en el cuarto. El abuelo está en el cuarto. (*The grandfather is in the bedroom.*)

Just one more. **La hija está en la sala. La hija está en la sala. La hija está en la sala.** (*The daughter is in the living room.*)

Muy bien, niños. (*Very good, children.*) Now we know where everyone is.

ESPAÑOL PARA TI, Level Three

END-OF-YEAR ASSESSMENT PAGE 3

The alphabet

Make sure the children have End-of-year Assessment pupil page 3 in front of them. Children are going to hear **la maestra** sing the "Alphabet Samba." They are to fill in the missing letters on their page as **la maestra** sings the song. Now play the audiotape, turning it off at the end of assessment activity 3.

Audio transcription:

Remember the "Alphabet Samba"? You're going to hear it now. Listen to it the first time through. The second time you hear it, fill in the letters that are missing on your paper. The third time, check over your answers. Be sure you have page 3 in front of you. Here's **la maestra**.

a, b, c
ch, d, e
f, g
h, i
j, k
l, ll, m, n, ñ, o
p, q
r, s
t, u
v
w
x
y
z

This time write in the missing letters as **la maestra** sings the song again.

Did you remember **las letras del alfabeto** (*the letters of the alphabet*)? Here is the "Alphabet Samba" one last time.

Muy bien, niños. (*Very good, children.*)

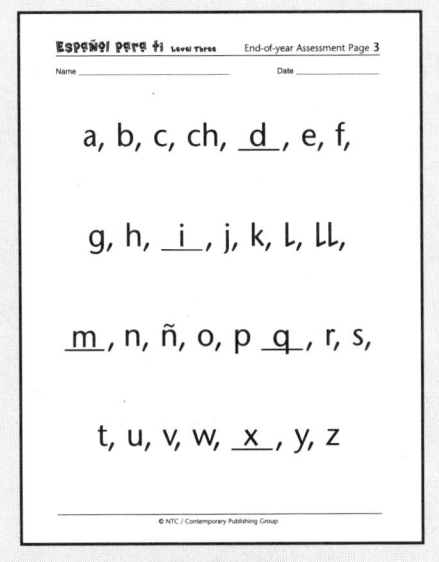

Espñol para ti Level Three — End-of-year Assessment Page 3
Name _____ Date _____

a, b, c, ch, _d_, e, f,

g, h, _i_, j, k, l, ll,

_m_, n, ñ, o, p _q_, r, s,

t, u, v, w, _x_, y, z

End-of-year Assessment
Page 3 Answer Key

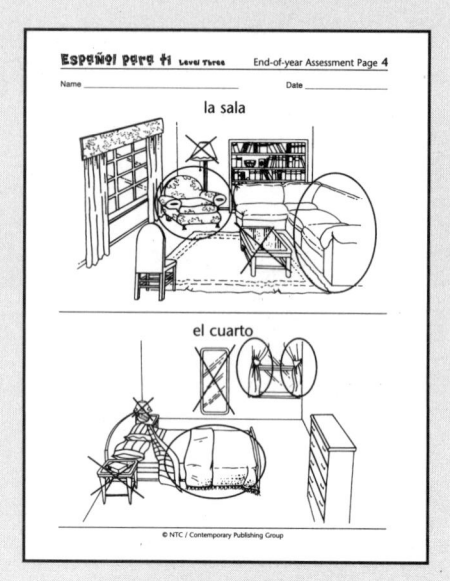

End-of-year Assessment
Page 4 Answer Key

END-OF-YEAR ASSESSMENT PAGE 4

Furniture

Make sure the children have End-of-year Assessment pupil page 4 in front of them. Point out that on the top half of the page is a picture of a living room and on the bottom half is a picture of a bedroom. Doña Elena is going shopping to redecorate her house. Children should circle each item she says she needs and cross out items she says she does not need. She will shop first for living room furnishings and then shop for her bedroom. The children will hear each segment three times with a pause in between. Now play the audiotape, turning it off at the end of assessment activity 4.

Audio transcription:

Niños, ¿vamos de compras? (*Children, shall we go shopping?*) As I shop, I'm going to mention things I need and things I don't need for my living room and then for my bedroom. You will circle the items I need and cross out those I don't need. Are you looking at the top drawing on your page? Here we go. I'll say each shopping segment three times.

This is a very nice store. They carry everything for the home. **Para la sala necesito un sofá.** (*For the living room I need a sofa.*) **Aquí está un sofá de color café.** (*Here is a brown sofa.*) **¡Perfecto!** (*Perfect!*) **Necesito también un sillón muy cómodo.** (*I also need a very comfortable armchair.*) **Este sillón es muy cómodo y no cuesta mucho.** (*This armchair is very comfortable and doesn't cost much.*) **Esta lámpara es muy bonita pero no necesito una lámpara.** (*This lamp is very pretty, but I don't need a lamp.*) **Y no necesito una mesa.** (*And I don't need a table.*)

[Above paragraph is repeated in its entirety two more times.]

Bueno. (*Good.*) **Vamos a comprar cosas para mi cuarto.** (*Let's shop for things for my bedroom.*)

Now let's move on to my bedroom. **Para mi cuarto necesito una cama.** (*For my bedroom, I need a bed.*) **¡Esta cama es muy grande!** (*This bed is very large!*) **Aquí está un espejo pero no necesito un espejo.** (*Here is a mirror, but I don't need a mirror.*) **¿Y qué más necesito?** (*And what else do I need?*) Hmmm, **no necesito una mesa para mi cuarto.** (*I don't need a table for my bedroom.*) **Ah, necesito cortinas y éstas son muy bonitas.** (*Ah, I need curtains and these are very pretty.*) **¿Necesito una lámpara?** (*Do I need a lamp?*) **No, yo no necesito una lámpara para mi cuarto.** (*No, I don't need a lamp for my bedroom.*)

[Above paragraph is repeated two more times.]

Bueno, niños. (*Good, children.*) **Adiós.** (*Good-bye.*)

ESPAÑOL PARA TI, Level Three

END-OF-YEAR ASSESSMENT PAGE 5

Kitchen appliances

Make sure the children have End-of-year Assessment pupil page 5 in front of them. Point out that on the page are all the kitchen appliances for which children have learned the Spanish words. Doña Elena needs new appliances. Children should circle the appliances doña Elena says she needs and cross out those she says she does <u>not</u> need. Now play the audiotape, turning it off at the end of assessment activity 5.

Audio transcription:

Niños (*Children*), my kitchen appliances are old and breaking down. **¡Vamos de compras!** (*Let's go shopping!*) Circle the appliances I say I need and cross out the ones I say I don't need.

Aquí está un refrigerador. (*Here is a refrigerator.*) **El refrigerador es de color blanco y es muy grande.** (*The refrigerator is white and very large.*) **Necesito un refrigerador.** (*I need a refrigerator.*)

El lavaplatos. (*The dishwasher.*) **Quiero un lavaplatos.** (*I want a dishwasher.*) **No tengo un lavaplatos.** (*I don't have a dishwasher.*) **¿Necesito un lavaplatos?** (*Do I need a dishwasher?*) **Sí, ¡necesito un lavaplatos!** (*Yes, I need a dishwasher.*)

El fregadero es muy grande. (*The sink is very large.*) **Pero no necesito un fregadero.** (*But I don't need a sink.*)

No necesito una estufa o un horno pero necesito un microondas. (*I don't need a stove or an oven, but I do need a microwave oven.*)

Y necesito también una lavadora. (*And I also need a washing machine.*) **¿Y la secadora?** (*And the dryer?*) **No, no necesito la secadora.** (*No, I don't need the dryer.*)

[The above statements are repeated as a whole two more times.]

I think that is enough shopping for today, **niños** (*children*). **¡Fantástico!** (*Fantastic!*)

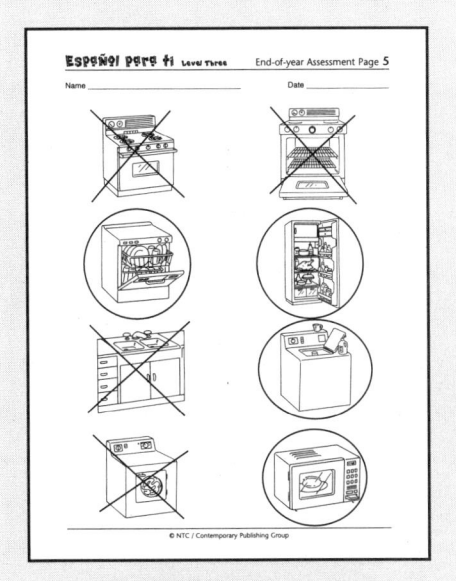

End-of-year Assessment Page 5 Answer Key

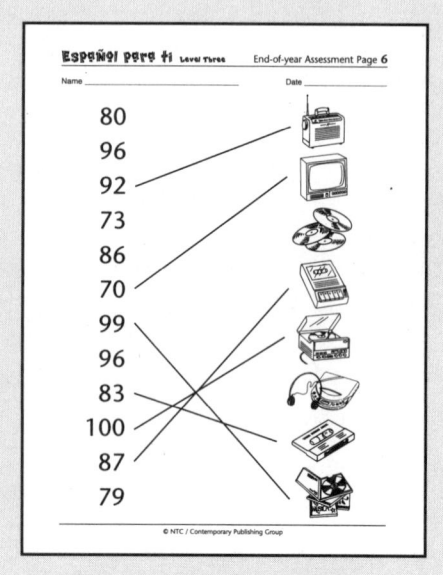

End-of-year Assessment Page 6

Big numbers and entertainment appliances

Make sure the children have End-of-year Assessment pupil page 6 in front of them. Point out that on the left side of the page are some big numbers and on the right side of the page are pictures of entertainment appliances. Doña Elena is going to say a big number followed by an entertainment appliance. Children should draw a line between the number and the entertainment appliance. Now play the audiotape, turning it off at the end of assessment activity 6.

Audio transcription:

Do you have page 6 in front of you, children? In this activity, I'm going to say a big number and then name an entertainment appliance. You will locate the number and the appliance I say and draw a line to connect them. I will say the number and the appliance three times. ¿Listos? (*Ready?*) Muy bien. (*Very good.*)

Noventa y dos, el radio. Noventa y dos, el radio. Noventa y dos, el radio. (*Ninety-two, the radio.*)

Are you done? Let's try another. **Ochenta y siete, la grabadora. Ochenta y siete, la grabadora. Ochenta y siete, la grabadora.** (*Eighty-seven, the cassette player.*)

Noventa y nueve, los discos CD. Noventa y nueve, los discos CD. Noventa y nueve, los discos CD. (*Ninety-nine, the CDs.*)

Ready for the next one? **Setenta, la televisión. Setenta, la televisión. Setenta, la televisión.** (*Seventy, the television.*) **¡Excelente, clase!** (*Excellent, class!*)

Ochenta y tres, la cinta. Ochenta y tres, la cinta. Ochenta y tres, la cinta. (*Eighty-three, the cassette.*)

And here's the last one. **Cien, el tocadiscos. Cien, el tocadiscos. Cien, el tocadiscos.** (*One hundred, the record player.*)

That was the last one. **Me gusta escuchar la música.** (*I like to listen to music.*) **¡Fantástico, niños!** (*Fantastic, children!*)

End-of-year Assessment Page 6 Answer Key

ESPAÑOL PARA TI, Level Three

END-OF-YEAR ASSESSMENT PAGE 7

Seasonal activities

Make sure the children have End-of-year Assessment pupil page 7 in front of them. Point out that each row shows Rosco and Dora involved in two seasonal activities. Doña Elena is going to talk with Rosco and Dora about what they like to do. For each row, children should circle the picture of the sport the puppet says he or she likes to do. Now play the audiotape, turning it off at the end of assessment activity 7.

Audio transcription:

¡Hola, clase! (*Hello, class!*) Are you ready with page 7? I'm going to ask our friends Rosco and Dora what they like to do. Listen carefully and circle what activity they say they like. Each conversation will be said three times.

Row 1. **Rosco, ¿qué quieres hacer?** (*What do you want to do?*)

(Rosco:) **Quiero jugar al fútbol.** (*I want to play soccer.*)

¿No quieres jugar al fútbol americano? (*You don't want to play football?*)

(Rosco:) **No, no quiero jugar al fútbol americano. Quiero jugar al fútbol.** (*No, I don't want to play football. I want to play soccer.*)

Muy bien, Rosco. (*Very good, Rosco.*) [Conversation is repeated two more times.]

Are you ready for row 2? Here we go. **Dora, ¿quieres esquiar?** (*Do you want to ski?*)

(Dora:) **No, no quiero esquiar. Quiero patinar.** (*No, I don't want to ski. I want to skate.*)

Bueno, Dora. (*Good, Dora.*) [Conversation is repeated two more times.]

Row 3. **Y Dora, ¿quieres jugar al tenis o quieres jugar al básquetbol?** (*And Dora, do you want to play tennis or do you want to play basketball?*)

(Dora:) **Quiero jugar al tenis. No me gusta el básquetbol. Me gusta el tenis.** (*I want to play tennis. I don't like basketball. I like tennis.*)

Muy bien, Dora. (*Very good, Dora.*) [Conversation is repeated two more times.]

Here's the last one. Row 4. **Y Rosco, ¿quieres saltar la cuerda o quieres jugar al béisbol?** (*Do you want to jump rope or do you want to play baseball?*)

(Rosco:) **No me gusta saltar la cuerda. No me gusta. Me gusta jugar al béisbol. Quiero jugar al béisbol.** (*I don't like to jump rope. I don't like [it]. I like to play baseball. I want to play baseball.*)

Bueno, Rosco. Te gusta jugar al béisbol. (*Good, Rosco. You like to play baseball.*) [Conversation is repeated two more times.]

¡Excelente, clase! (*Excellent, class!*) It's always fun to talk with Rosco and Dora.

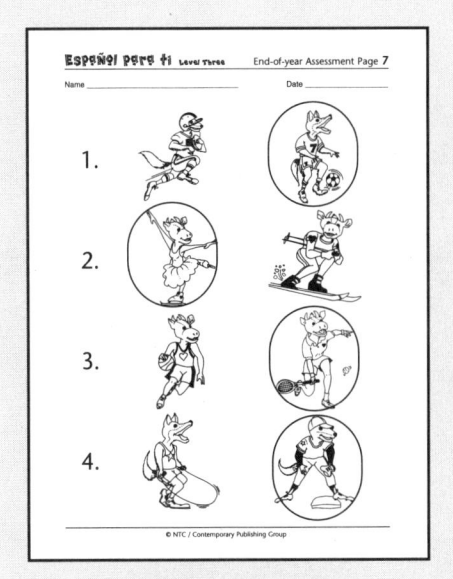

End-of-year Assessment Page 7 Answer Key

Teacher's Resource Book

END-OF-YEAR ASSESSMENT PAGE 8

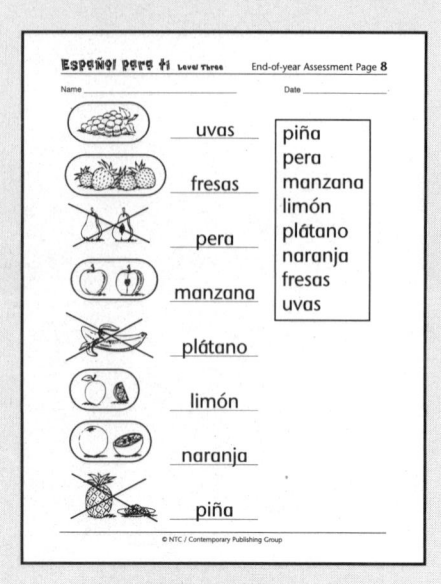

(No) Me gusta (I [don't] like), fruits, and writing

Make sure the children have End-of-year Assessment pupil page 8 in front of them. Point out that on the left side of the page are all the fruits for which the children have learned the Spanish words. Doña Elena is going to tell them what fruits she likes and doesn't like. The children will circle the fruits she likes and cross out the ones she doesn't like. Then, using the names of the fruits in the box on the right, the children will write the name of each fruit on the line next to the fruit. Now play the audiotape, turning it off at the end of assessment activity 8. Allow children time to write all the fruit names before continuing with assessment activity 9.

Audio transcription:

Children, do you like fruit? **Me gustan mucho las frutas.** (*I like fruit very much.*) I'm going to tell you what fruits I like and what fruits I don't like. You should circle the pictures of the fruits I like and cross out the ones I don't like. Let's begin.

Me gustan las uvas. Me gustan las uvas. Me gustan las uvas. (*I like the grapes.*)

Las fresas son de color rojo. (*The strawberries are red.*) **Me gustan mucho las fresas. Me gustan mucho las fresas. Me gustan mucho las fresas.** (*I like strawberries very much.*)

¿La pera? No me gusta la pera. No me gusta la pera. No me gusta la pera. (*The pear? I don't like the pear.*)

Pero me gusta la manzana. Me gusta la manzana. Me gusta la manzana. (*But I like the apple.*)

No me gusta el plátano. No me gusta el plátano. No me gusta el plátano. (*I don't like the banana.*)

Me gusta el limón y me gusta la naranja. Me gusta el limón y me gusta la naranja. Me gusta el limón y me gusta la naranja. (*I like the lemon and I like the orange.*)

Pero no me gusta la piña. No me gusta la piña. No me gusta la piña. (*I don't like the pineapple.*)

Now, children, using the words in the box as a guide, write the Spanish name of each fruit on the line next to it. **¡Perfecto, clase!** (*Perfect, class!*)

End-of-year Assessment Page 8 Answer Key

ESPAÑOL PARA TI, Level Three

END-OF-YEAR ASSESSMENT PAGE 9

Mealtimes and foods

Make sure the children have End-of-year Assessment pupil page 9 in front of them. Point out that on the left side of their page are three pictures, each representing a time of day. On the right side are pictures of various foods whose names they know in Spanish. Doña Elena is going to talk about what she eats for each meal. The children should draw lines from the picture of the time of day when doña Elena eats the meal to all the foods she says she is going to eat. Doña Elena will describe each meal three times. Remind the children to listen the first time, mark the answer the second time, and check their answer the third time. Now play the audiotape, turning it off at the end of assessment activity 9.

Audio transcription:

¡Hola, niños! (*Hello, children!*) Are you ready with page 9? Tengo hambre. (*I'm hungry.*) I'm going to tell you what I eat for each meal. You will draw a line from the picture that represents the time of day when I eat the meal to the foods I say I'm going to eat for that meal. I'll begin with the first meal of the day.

Para el desayuno me gusta comer cereal y pan tostado, y me gusta tomar una taza de té. (*For breakfast I like to eat cereal and toast and I like to drink a cup of tea.*) (3x)

Let's try another. ¿Listos? (*Ready?*) **Para el almuerzo me gusta la sopa y las galletas. Y tomo un vaso de leche.** (*For lunch I like soup and crackers. And I drink a glass of milk.*) (3x)

Only one meal left in the day. **Para la cena como pollo con arroz y tomo un vaso de leche.** (*For dinner I eat chicken with rice and I drink a glass of milk.*) (3x)

After such a big meal, **tengo sueño.** (*I'm sleepy.*)

Adiós, niños. (*Good-bye, children.*)

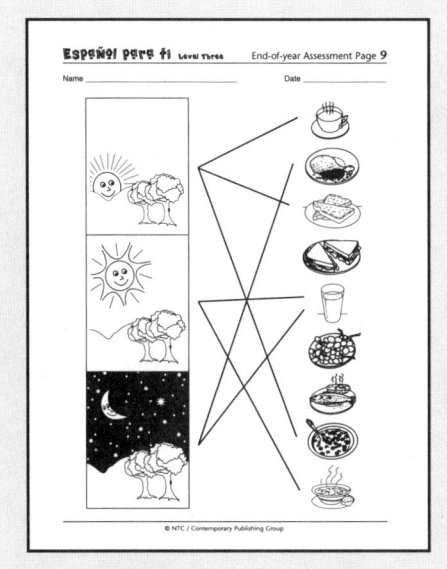

End-of-year Assessment
Page 9 Answer Key

Teacher's Resource Book

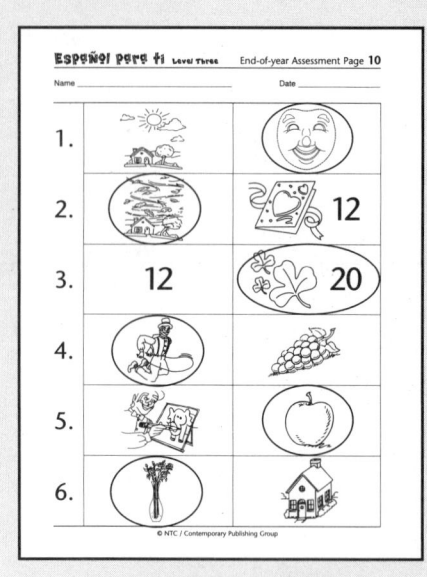

End-of-year Assessment
Page 10 Answer Key

END-OF-YEAR ASSESSMENT PAGE 10

Identifying various questions

Make sure the children have End-of-year Assessment pupil page 10 in front of them. Remind children that they know how to answer many questions. For each row, doña Elena will ask a question and children should circle the picture that best fits or answers the question. Now play the audiotape, turning it off at the end of assessment activity 10.

Audio transcription:

Are you looking at page 10? Let's have some fun finding answers to questions. Circle the picture that answers each question I ask you.

Here we go with row 1. ¿Cómo estás tú? ¿Cómo estás tú? ¿Cómo estás tú? (*How are you?*)

Let's go to row 2. ¿Qué tiempo hace? ¿Qué tiempo hace? ¿Qué tiempo hace? (*What's the weather like?*)

Now row 3. ¿Cuál es la fecha? ¿Cuál es la fecha? ¿Cuál es la fecha? (*What's the date?*)

Now row 4. ¿Qué quieres hacer? ¿Qué quieres hacer? ¿Qué quieres hacer? (*What do you want to do?*)

Now let's do row 5. ¿Qué quieres comer? ¿Qué quieres comer? ¿Qué quieres comer? (*What do you want to eat?*)

Now row 6. ¿Qué pones en la mesa? ¿Qué pones en la mesa? ¿Qué pones en la mesa? (*What do you put on the table?*)

¡Qué bueno, clase! (*What a good job, class!*) ¡Adiós! (*Goodbye!*)

ESPAÑOL PARA TI, Level Three

Español para ti Level Three

End-of-year Assessment Page **1**

Name _____   Date _____

1.

2.

3.

4.

5.

6.

© NTC / Contemporary Publishing Group

Español para ti   Level Three

End-of-year Assessment Page **2**

Name _____   Date _____

© NTC / Contemporary Publishing Group

Español para ti Level Three
End-of-year Assessment Page 3

Name _____ Date _____

a, b, c, ch, ___, e, f,

g, h, ___, j, k, l, ll,

___, n, ñ, o, p ___, r, s,

t, u, v, w, ___, y, z

© NTC / Contemporary Publishing Group

Español para ti Level Three

End-of-year Assessment Page **4**

Name _____   Date _____

la sala

el cuarto

© NTC / Contemporary Publishing Group

Español para ti Level Three   End-of-year Assessment Page 5

Name _____   Date _____

Español para ti Level Three

End-of-year Assessment Page **6**

Name _____

Date _____

80

96

92

73

86

70

99

96

83

100

87

79

Español para ti Level Three — End-of-year Assessment Page 7

Name _____   Date _____

1.

2.

3.

4.

Español para ti Level Three   End-of-year Assessment Page **8**

Name _____ Date _____

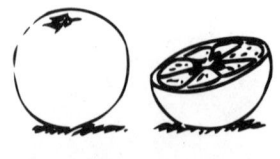

_____

_____

_____

_____

_____

_____

_____

_____

| piña |
| pera |
| manzana |
| limón |
| plátano |
| naranja |
| fresas |
| uvas |

© NTC / Contemporary Publishing Group

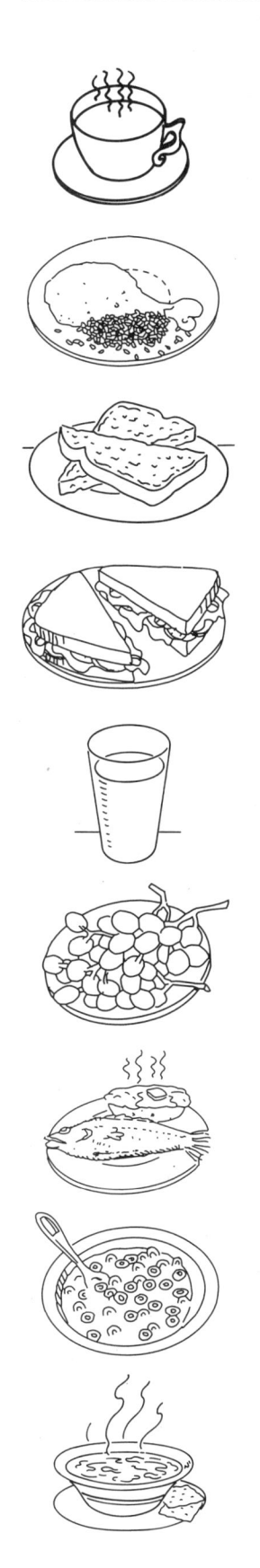

Español para ti Level Three End-of-year Assessment Page 9

Name _____ Date _____

Español para ti Level Three

End-of-year Assessment Page **10**

Name _____ Date _____

1.			
2.			 12
3.	12		 20
4.			
5.			
6.			

© NTC / Contemporary Publishing Group

Rubric for Holistic Assessment

Below is a simple rubric for gauging children's participation and progress at any time during the course. Check the appropriate box under each relevant item, and add comments if you wish.

Child's Name _____ Date _____

	NEVER	SOMETIMES	ALWAYS	NOT APPLICABLE
1. Listens but does not respond orally.	❏	❏	❏	❏

Comment: _____

2. Listens and repeats.	❏	❏	❏	❏

Comment: _____

3. Sings along with videotape.	❏	❏	❏	❏

Comment: _____

4. Sings along with Song Cassette.	❏	❏	❏	❏

Comment: _____

5. Responds to commands appropriately.	❏	❏	❏	❏

Comment: _____

6. Answers nonpersonal questions.	❏	❏	❏	❏

Comment: _____

7. Answers personal questions.	❏	❏	❏	❏

Comment: _____

8. Participates in Activity Cassette activities.	❏	❏	❏	❏

Comment: _____

9. Uses appropriate body language.	❏	❏	❏	❏

Comment: _____

10. Uses **tú** and **usted** correctly.	❏	❏	❏	❏

Comment: _____

11. Is willing or volunteers to speak Spanish.	❏	❏	❏	❏

Comment: _____

12. Uses context to figure out unfamiliar words.	❏	❏	❏	❏

Comment: _____

13. Can follow conversation and consecutive sentences.	❏	❏	❏	❏

Comment: _____

Sample Comments for Rubric

Repeats (more) easily.
Pronunciation seems to be (more) accurate.
Uses body language or props as appropriate to help remember song lyrics.
Is able to sing (some/more/all of) the song(s).
Volunteers to lead *Warm-up* and/or *Closing* activity.

Number cards

$$\frac{1}{2}$$

© NTC / Contemporary Publishing Group

3

4

5

6

© NTC / Contemporary Publishing Group

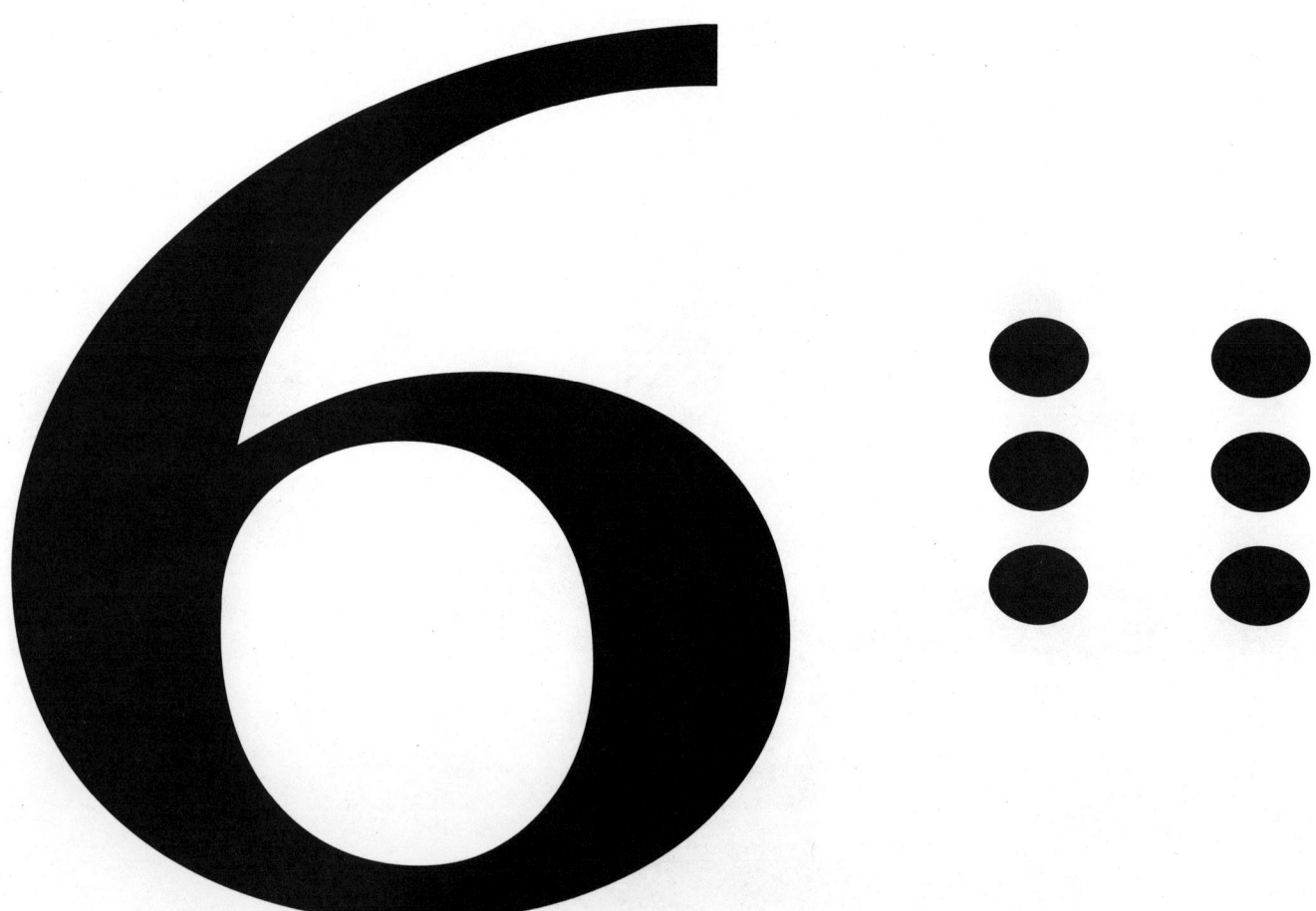

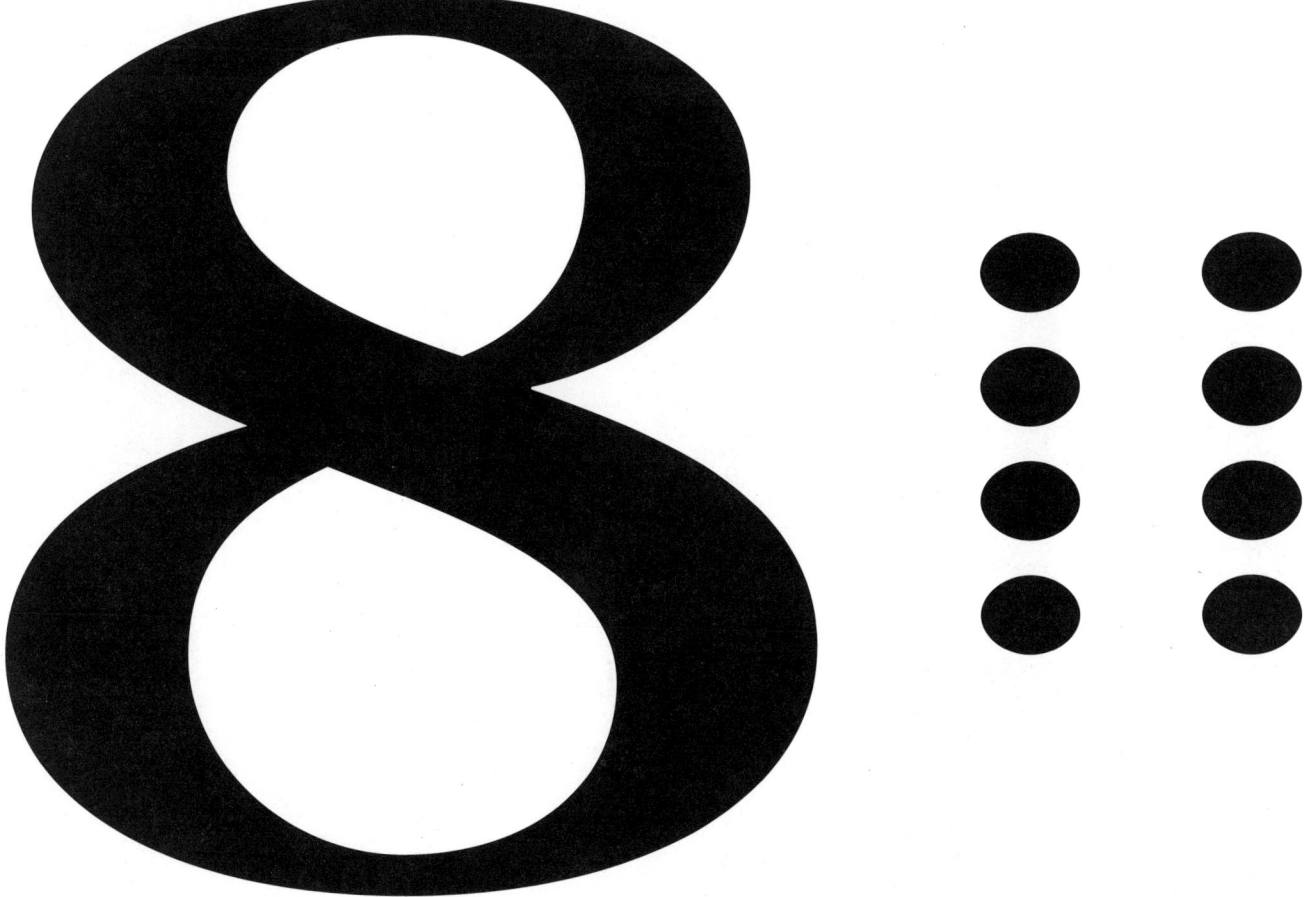

7

8

9

10

© NTC / Contemporary Publishing Group

11
12

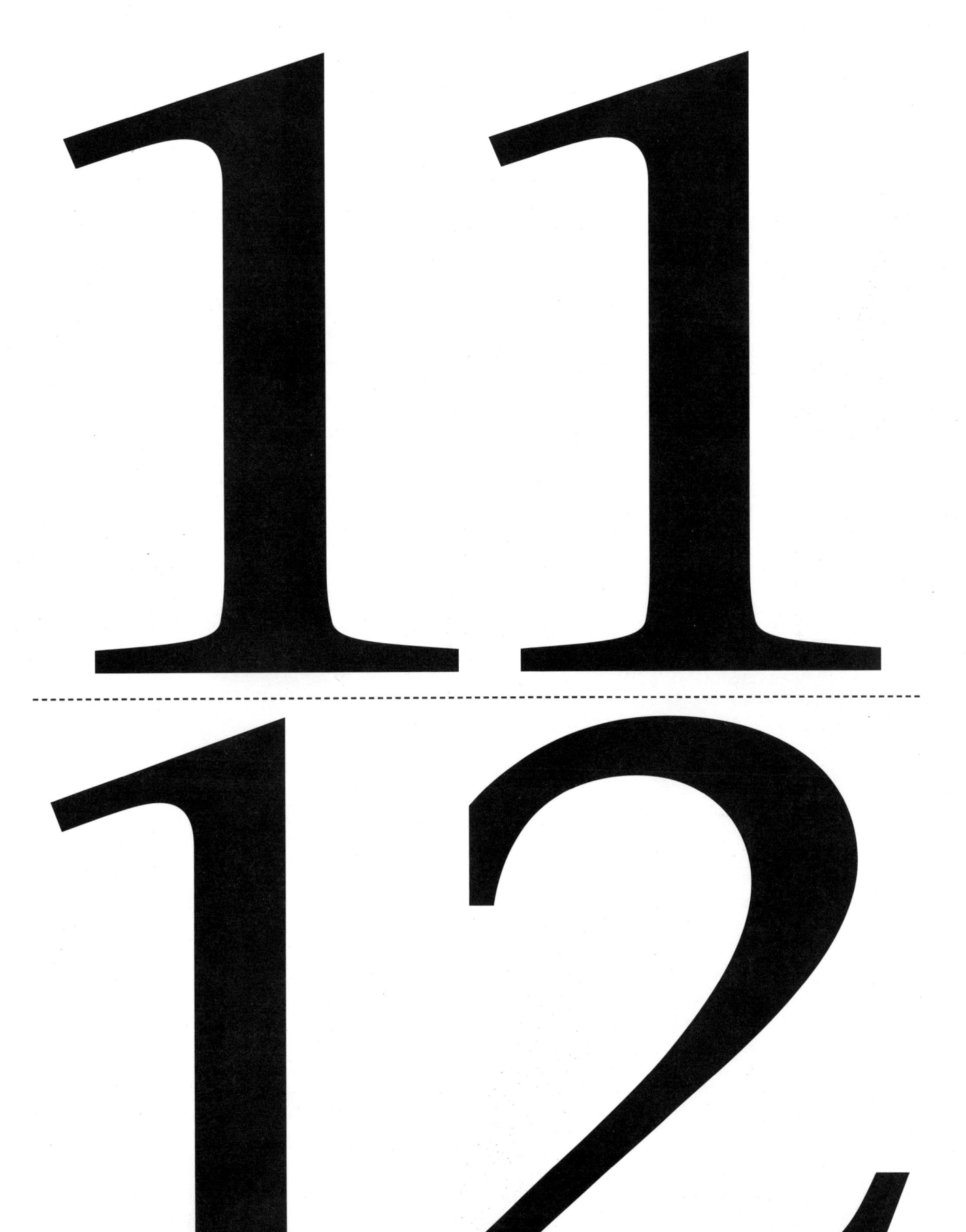

13

14

© NTC / Contemporary Publishing Group

15

16

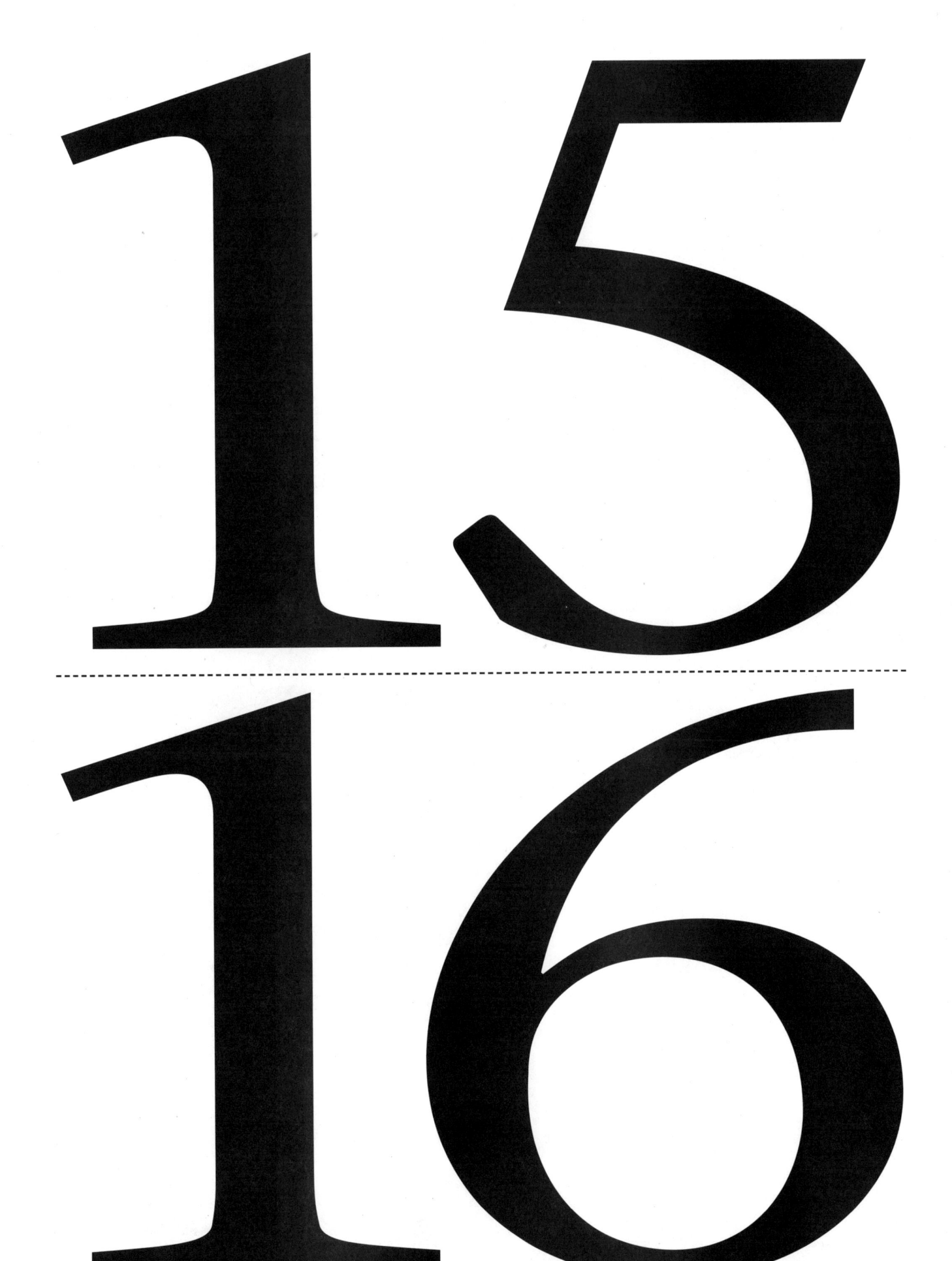

© NTC / Contemporary Publishing Group

17

18

© NTC / Contemporary Publishing Group

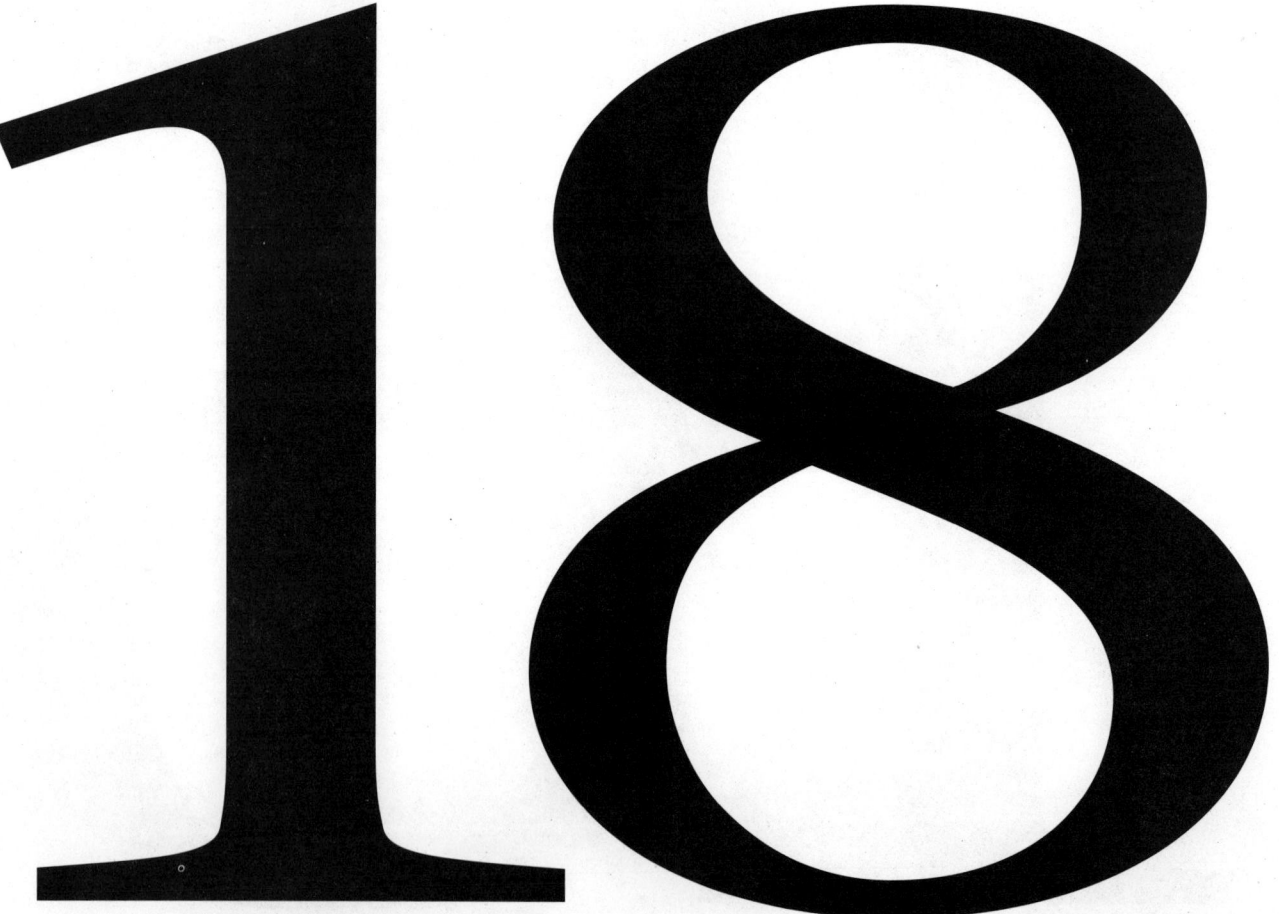

19
20

© NTC / Contemporary Publishing Group

10
20

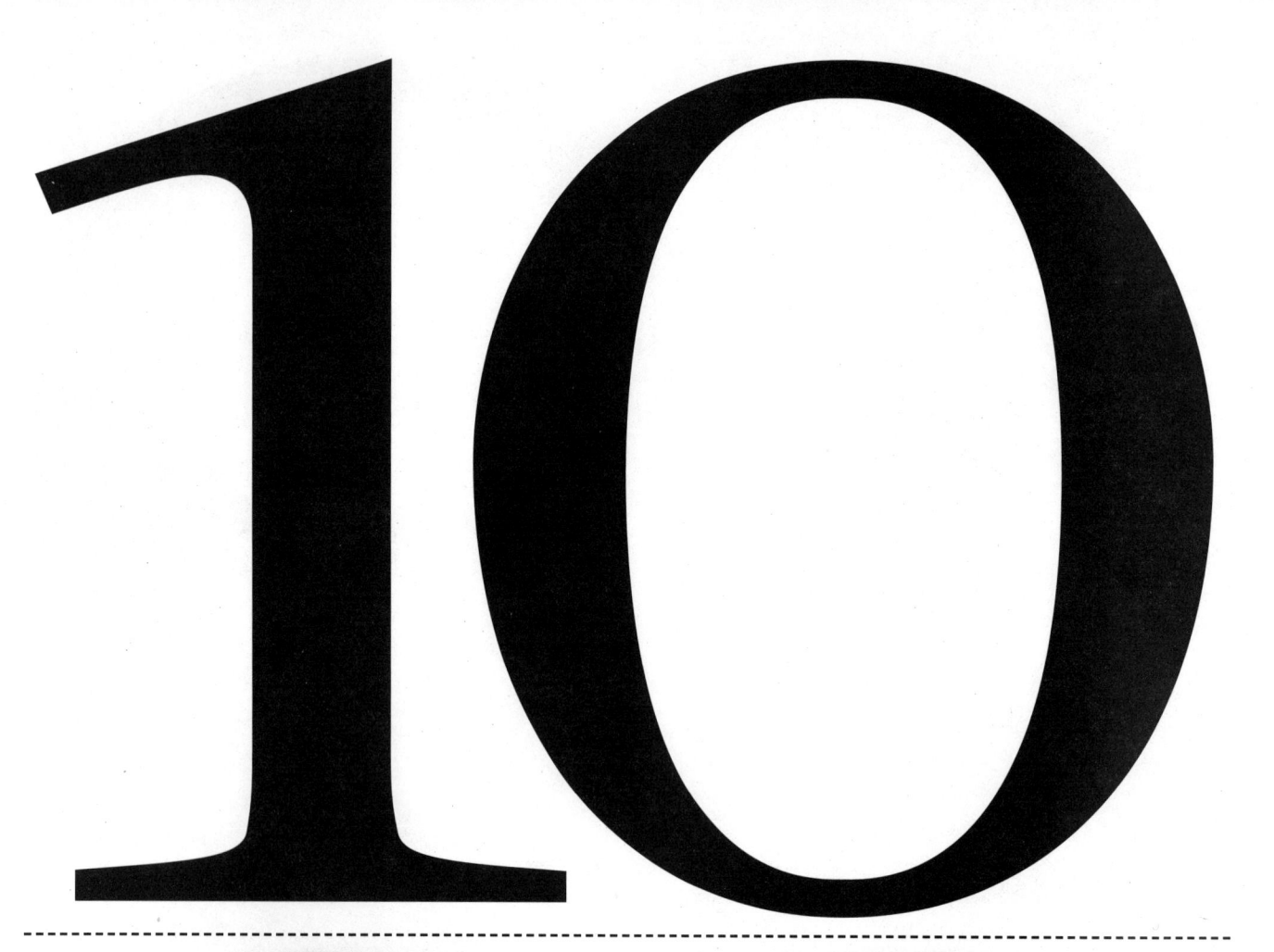

© NTC / Contemporary Publishing Group

30
40

© NTC / Contemporary Publishing Group

50

60

© NTC / Contemporary Publishing Group

70

80

© NTC / Contemporary Publishing Group

90
100

© NTC / Contemporary Publishing Group

Letter cards

Vowel Word Card

A MAPA

E PEPE

I LILI

O ROJO

U CUCÚ

© NTC / Contemporary Publishing Group

Alphabet Chart

a	j	r
b	k	s
c	l	t
ch	ll	u
d	m	v
e	n	w
f	ñ	x
g	o	y
h	p	z
i	q	

© NTC / Contemporary Publishing Group

Vowel Card

a

e

© NTC / Contemporary Publishing Group

Vowel Card

i

---

o

© NTC / Contemporary Publishing Group

Vowel Card

u

© NTC / Contemporary Publishing Group

Alphabet Cards

a

b

© NTC / Contemporary Publishing Group

C

ch

d

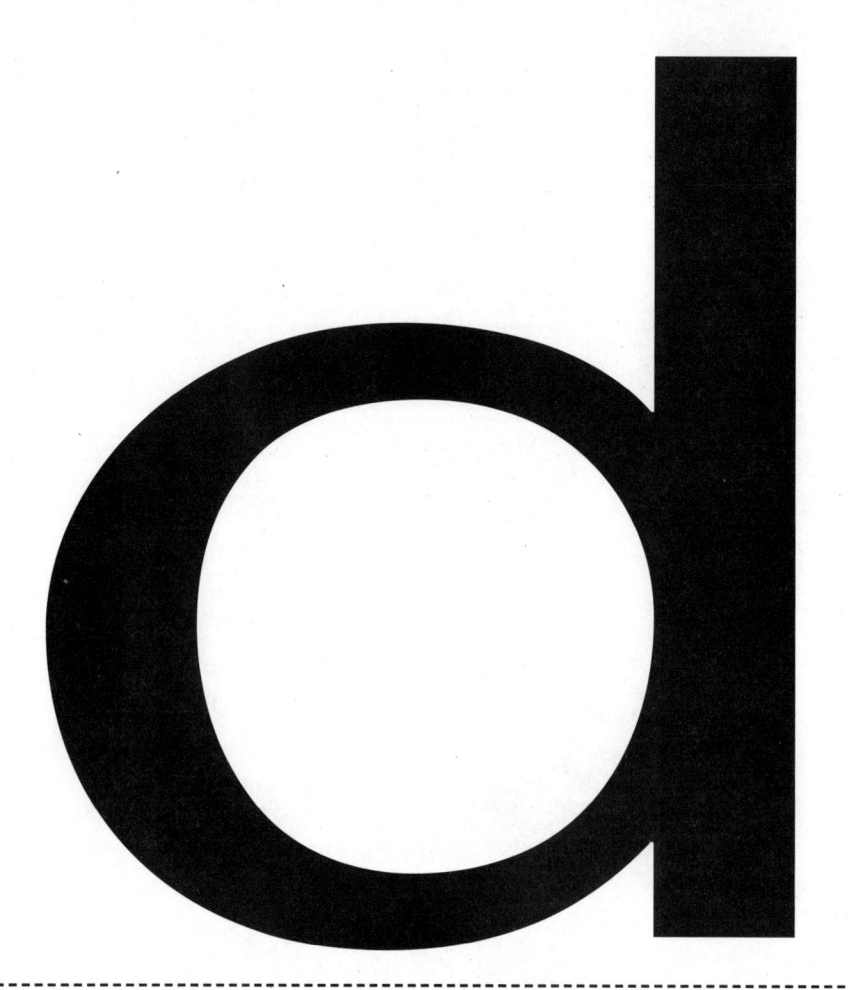

e

© NTC / Contemporary Publishing Group

f

g

h
i

© NTC / Contemporary Publishing Group

j

k

© NTC / Contemporary Publishing Group

m

n

ñ

o

p

q

© NTC / Contemporary Publishing Group

r

s

t

u

V w

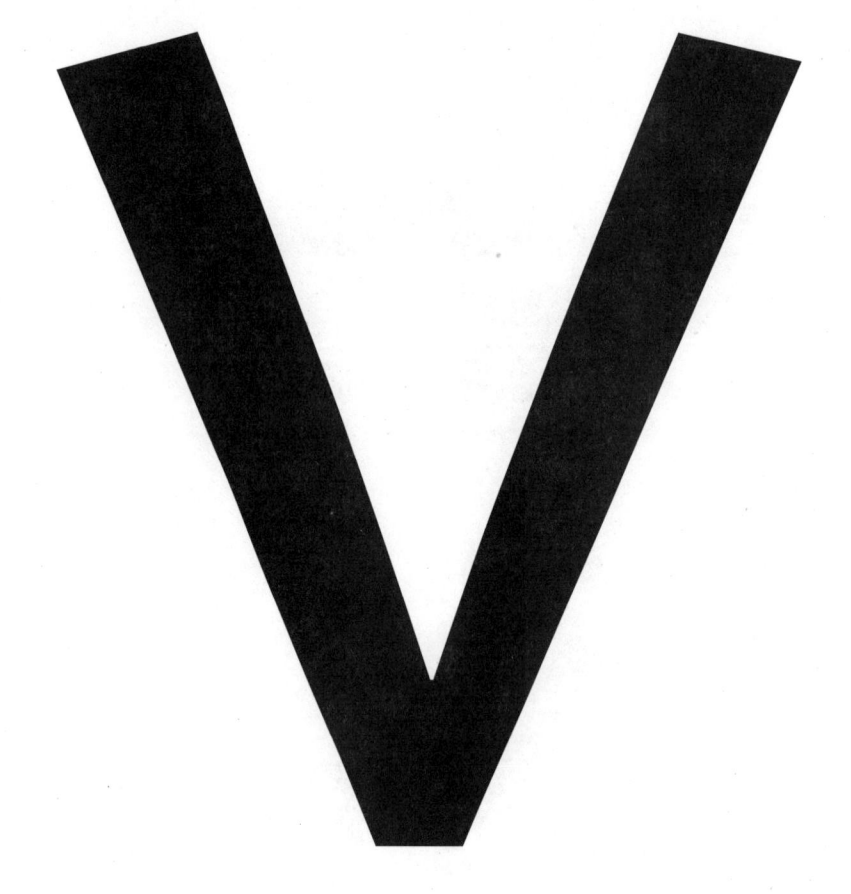

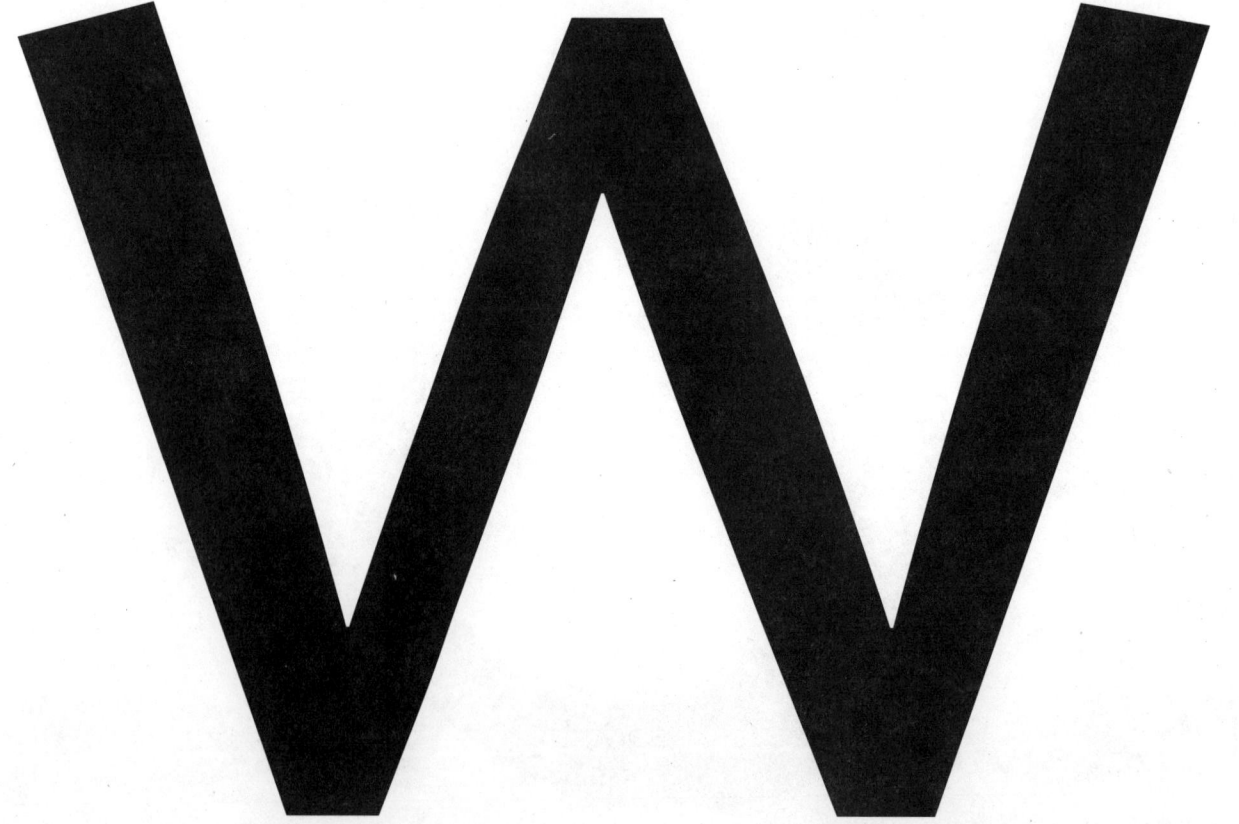

x

y

© NTC / Contemporary Publishing Group

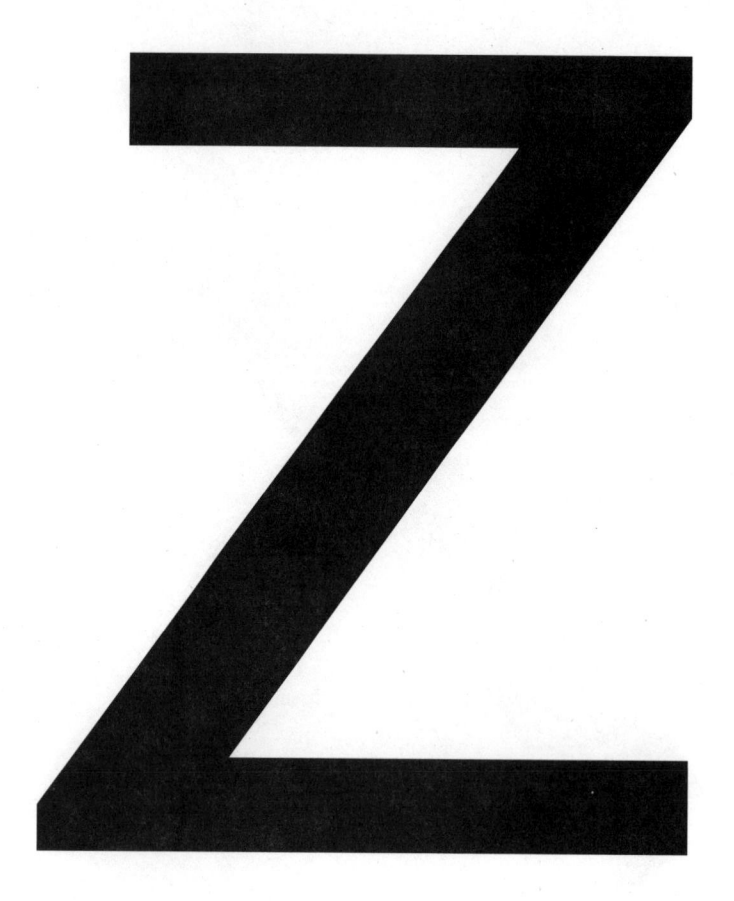

Z

Blockline Masters

Español para ti Level Three

Blackline Master **1A**

Rosco

Dora

Jorge

Ñico

© NTC / Contemporary Publishing Group

Español para ti Level Three

Blackline Master **2A**

☆ # _____

◯ # _____

🚗 # _____

✈ # _____

♡ # _____

✂------------------------------

1. 14   9   4   18

2. 16   8   17   6

3. 5   15   7   3

4. 20   12   2   19

5. 3   20   13   11

© NTC / Contemporary Publishing Group

Español para ti Level Three

Blackline Master **2C-1**

© NTC / Contemporary Publishing Group

Español para ti Level Three

Blackline Master **2C-2**

© NTC / Contemporary Publishing Group

Español para ti Level Three

Blackline Master 2C-3

Español para ti Level Three

Blackline Master **3C**

© NTC / Contemporary Publishing Group

Español para ti Level Three   Blackline Master **4A**

1.

2.

3.

4.

© NTC / Contemporary Publishing Group

Español para ti Level Three

Blackline Master 4C

Partner A

- ★ ____21____ 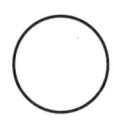
- ○ _____
- 🚗 ____10____ 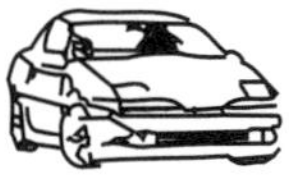 
- ✈ _____
- ♥ ____40____ 
- ☎ _____

✂ -

Partner B

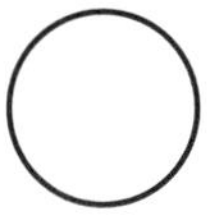

- ★ _____
- ○ ____35____
- 🚗 _____
- ✈ ____25____  
- ♥ _____
- ☎ ____16____  

© NTC / Contemporary Publishing Group

Español para ti Level Three

Blackline Master **7A**

1.

2.

3.

4.

© NTC / Contemporary Publishing Group

Español para ti Level Three

Blackline Master **8A**

1.  
2.  
3.  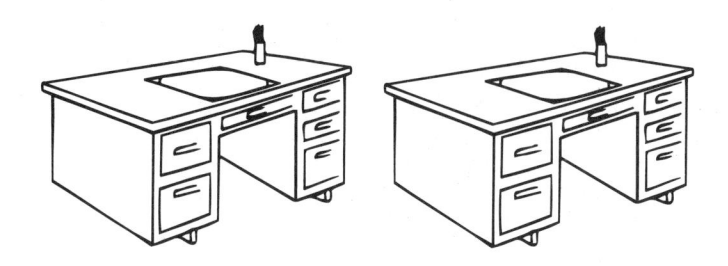
4.  
5.

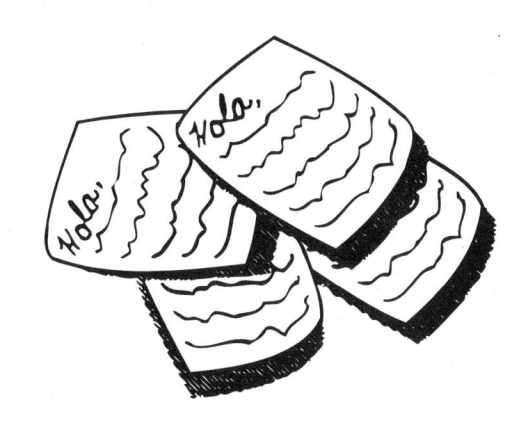

© NTC / Contemporary Publishing Group

Español para ti Level Three

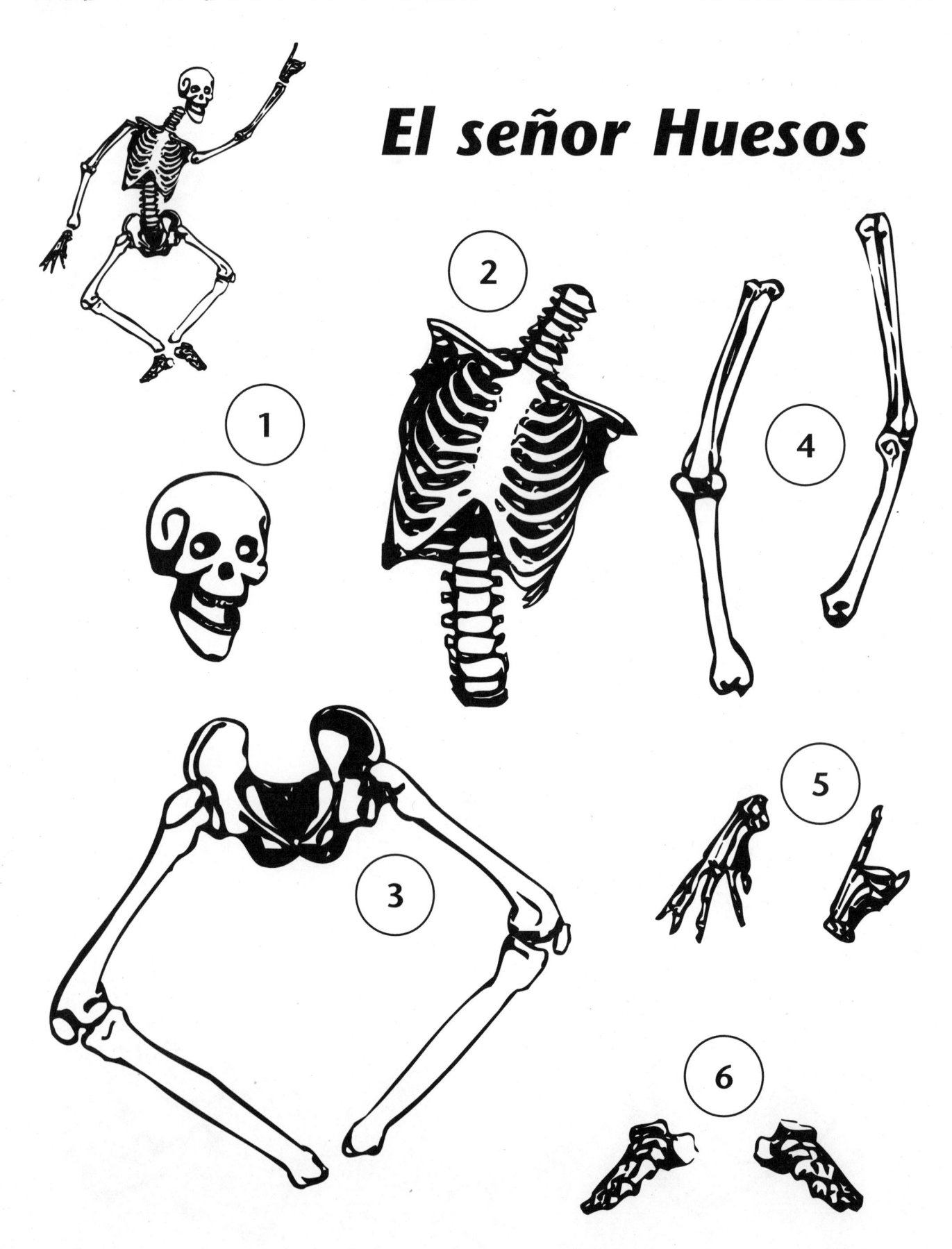

Blackline Master **9B**

El señor Huesos

1
2
3
4
5
6

© NTC / Contemporary Publishing Group

Español para ti Level Three

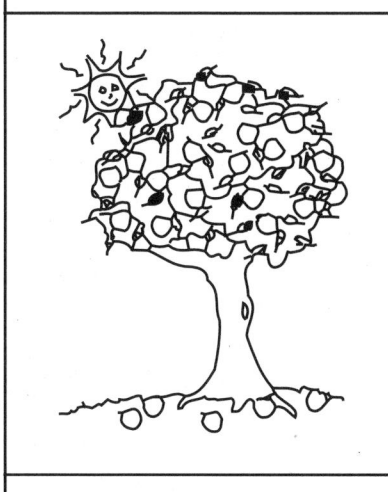

Blackline Master 10A

© NTC / Contemporary Publishing Group

Español para ti Level Three

Blackline Master 11B

© NTC / Contemporary Publishing Group

Español para ti Level Three

Blackline Master **12C**

© NTC / Contemporary Publishing Group

Español para ti Level Three

Blackline Master **17B**

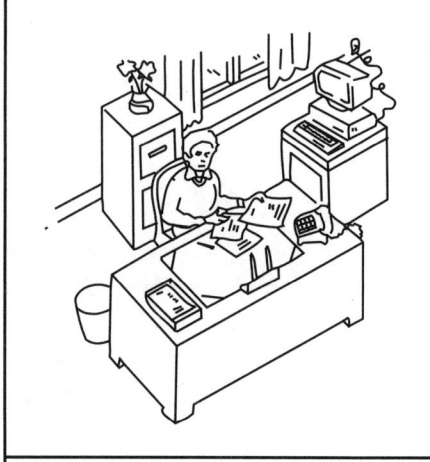

© NTC / Contemporary Publishing Group

Las vocales

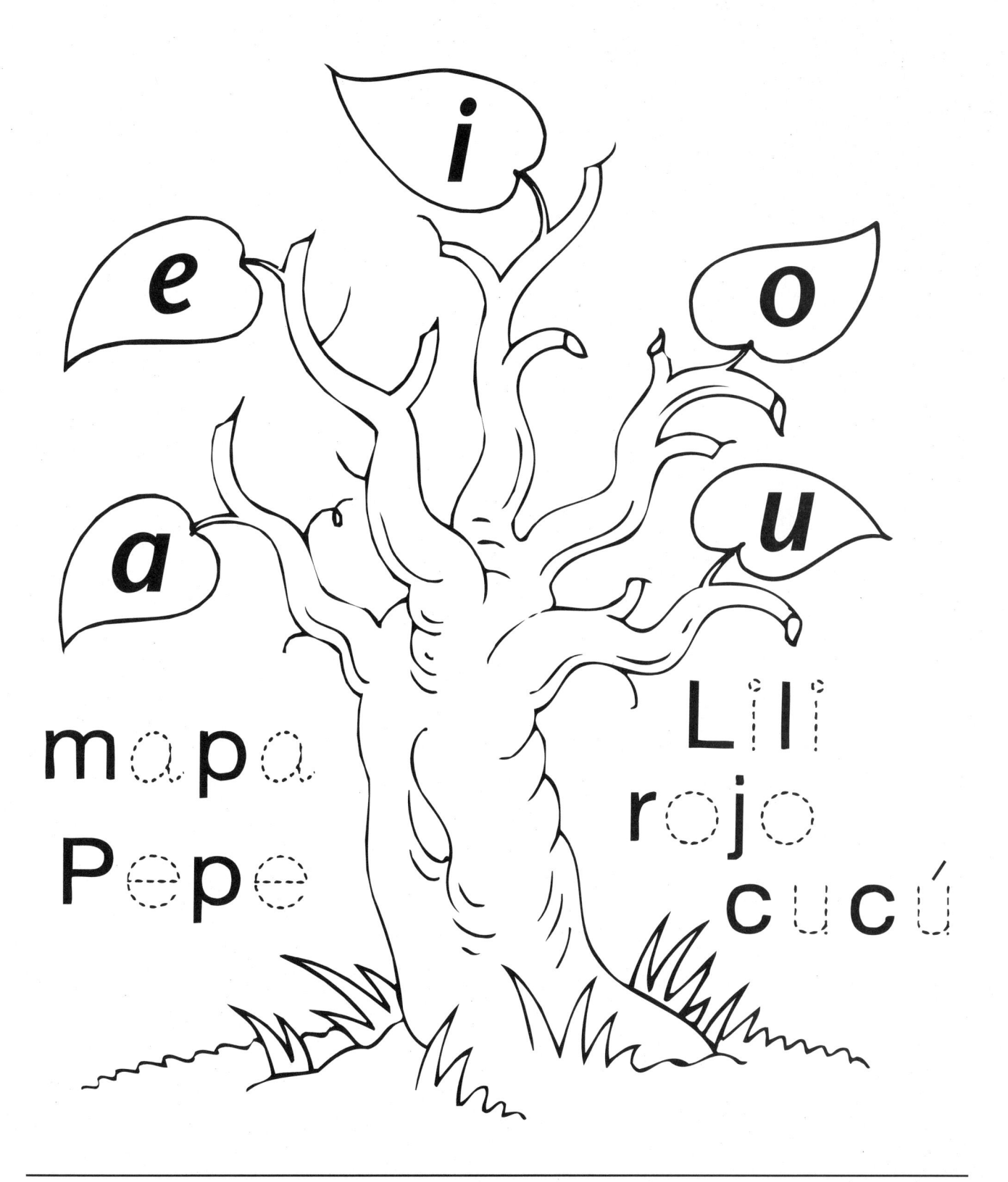

a e i o u

mapa
Pepe

Lili
rojo
cucú

Español para ti Level Three

Blackline Master 20B

1.   30
  + 20
  ―――

2.   70
  − 50
  ―――

3.   22
  + 17
  ―――

4.   55
  + 12
  ―――

5.   33
  + 6
  ―――

6.   15
  − 5
  ―――

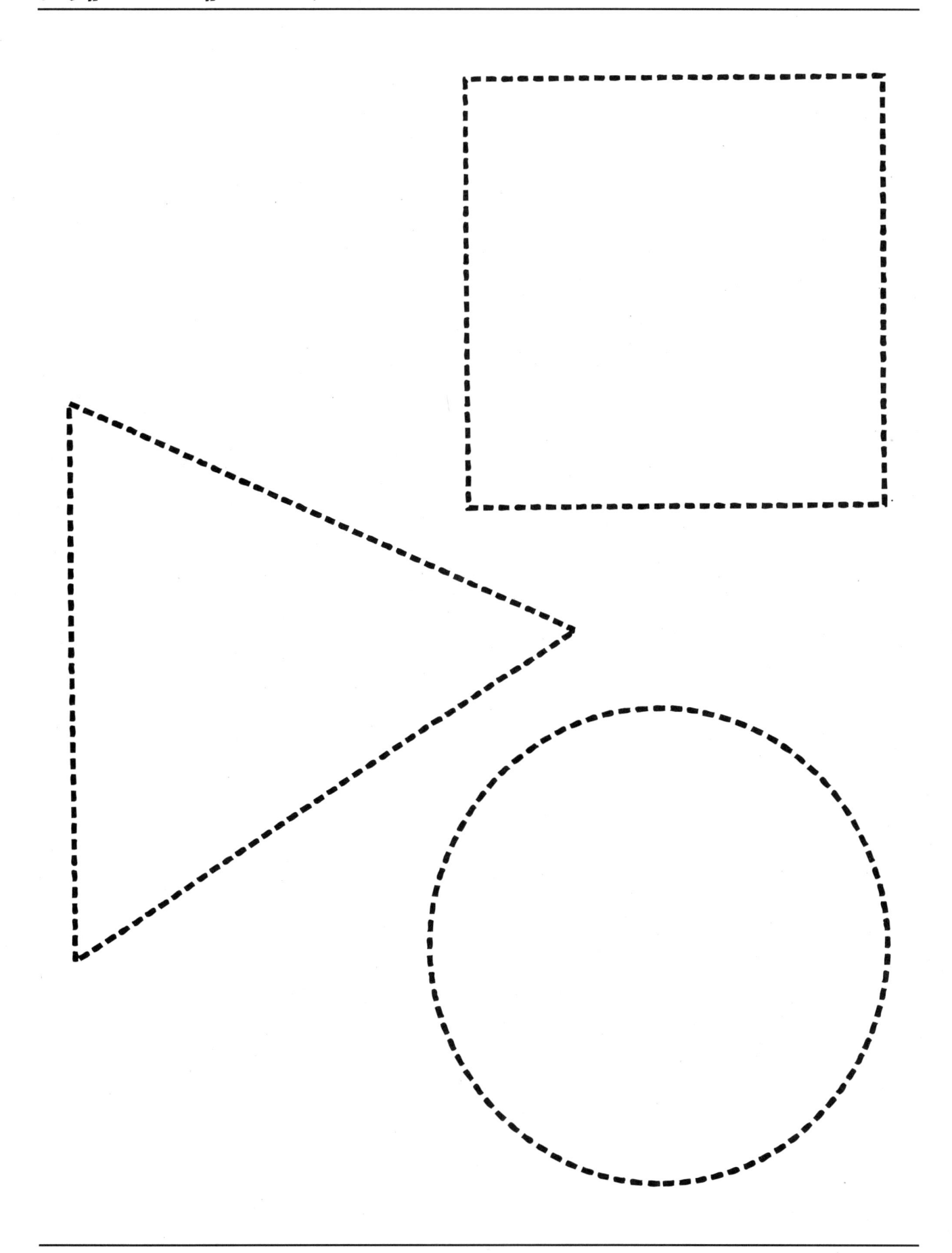

Español para ti Level Three

Blackline Master **21A**

© NTC / Contemporary Publishing Group

Español para ti Level Three

Blackline Master **21B**

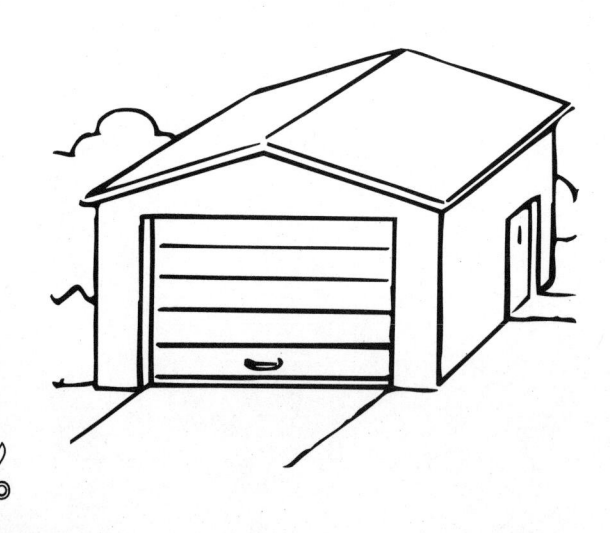

© NTC / Contemporary Publishing Group

1. l_nes

2. m_rtes

3. miérc__les

4. juev__s

5. viern__s

6. sábad__

7. dom__ngo

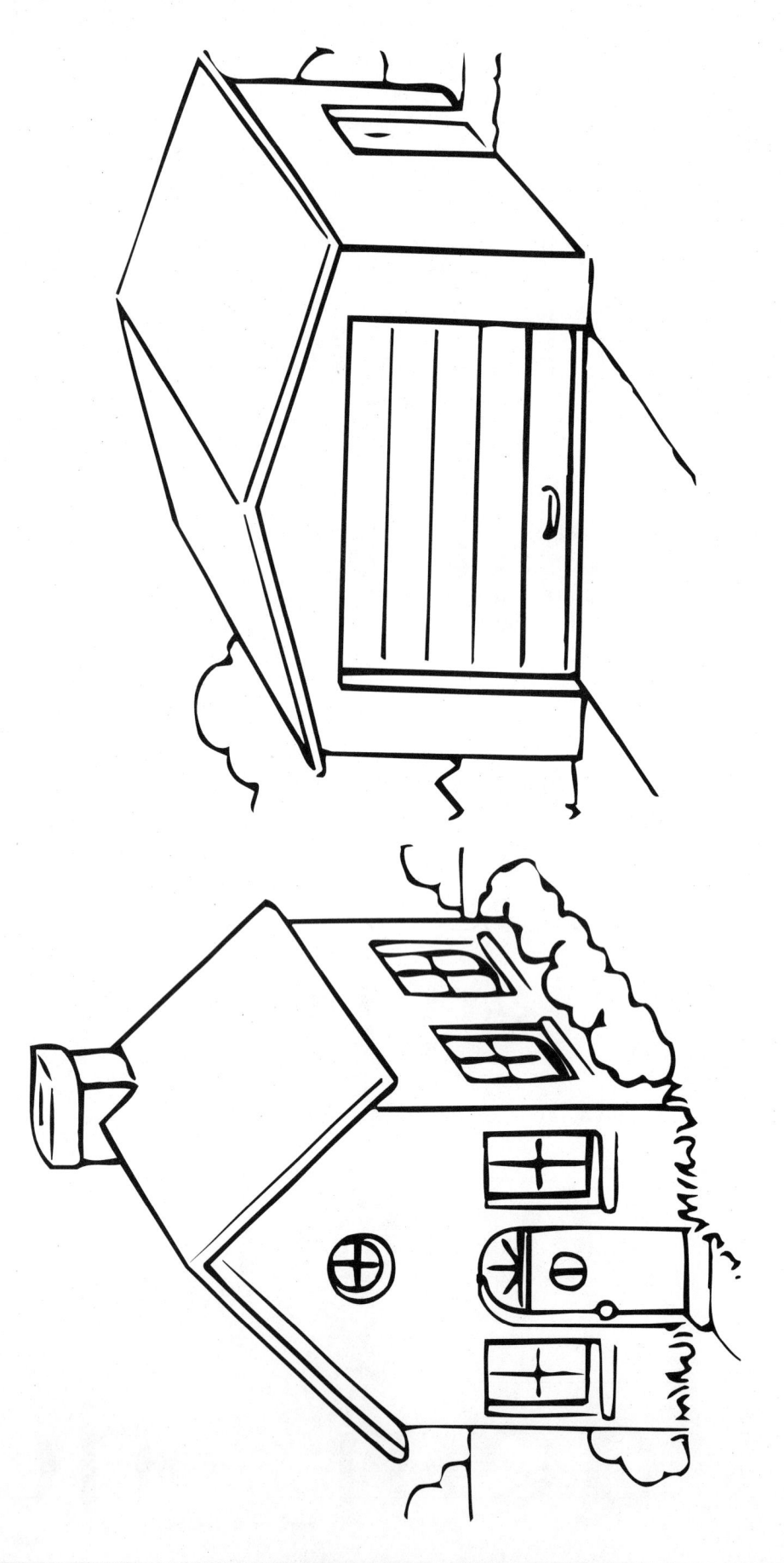

Español para ti Level Three

Blackline Master 23A

© NTC / Contemporary Publishing Group

Las vocales

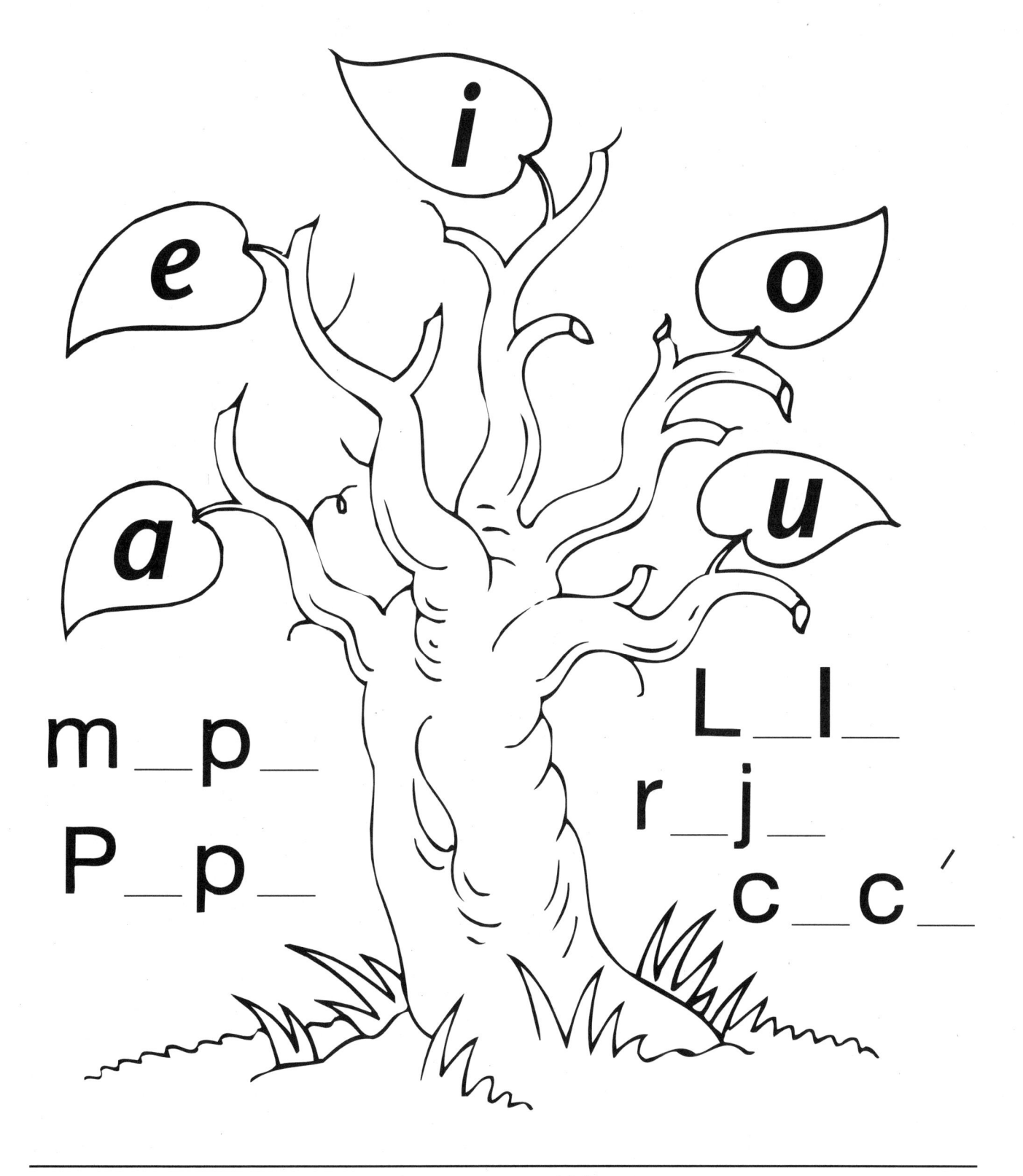

Español para ti Level Three — Blackline Master **23B**

i

e

o

a

u

m_p_

P_p_

L_l_

r_j_

c_c_´

© NTC / Contemporary Publishing Group

Español para ti Level Three

Blackline Master **24A**

© NTC / Contemporary Publishing Group

1. 14
   + 6
   ───

2. 80
   − 40
   ────

3. 70
   + 10
   ────

4. 36
   + 3
   ───

5. 74
   + 4
   ───

Español para ti Level Three

Blackline Master **27C**

1. abu__lo

2. abu__la

3. p__pá

4. m__má

5. herman__

6. herman__

© NTC / Contemporary Publishing Group

Español para ti Level Three Blackline Master **28A**

A.

1. el 6 de

2. el 20 de

3. el 31 de

B.

1. ___año

2. ___asa

3. c___rdo

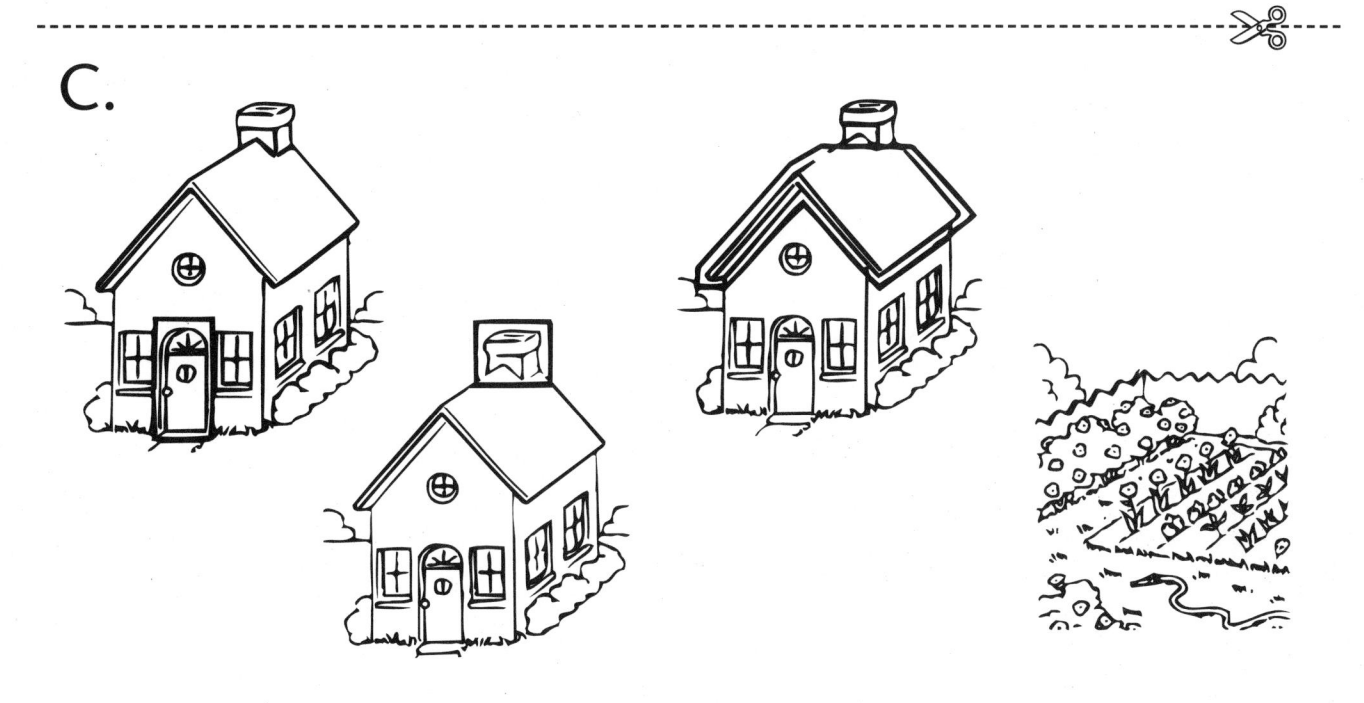

C.

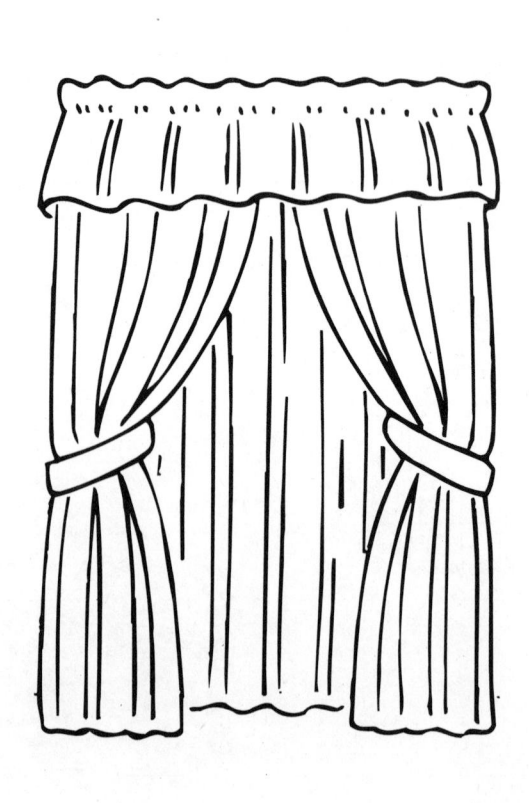

Español para ti — Level Three

Blackline Master **34B**

© NTC / Contemporary Publishing Group

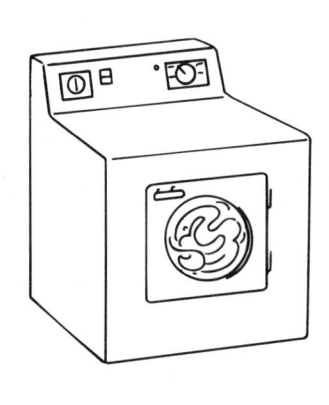

Español para ti Level Three

Blackline Master 38A

© NTC / Contemporary Publishing Group

Español para ti Level Three

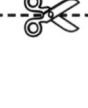

Blackline Master **46A-1**

© NTC / Contemporary Publishing Group

Español para ti Level Three

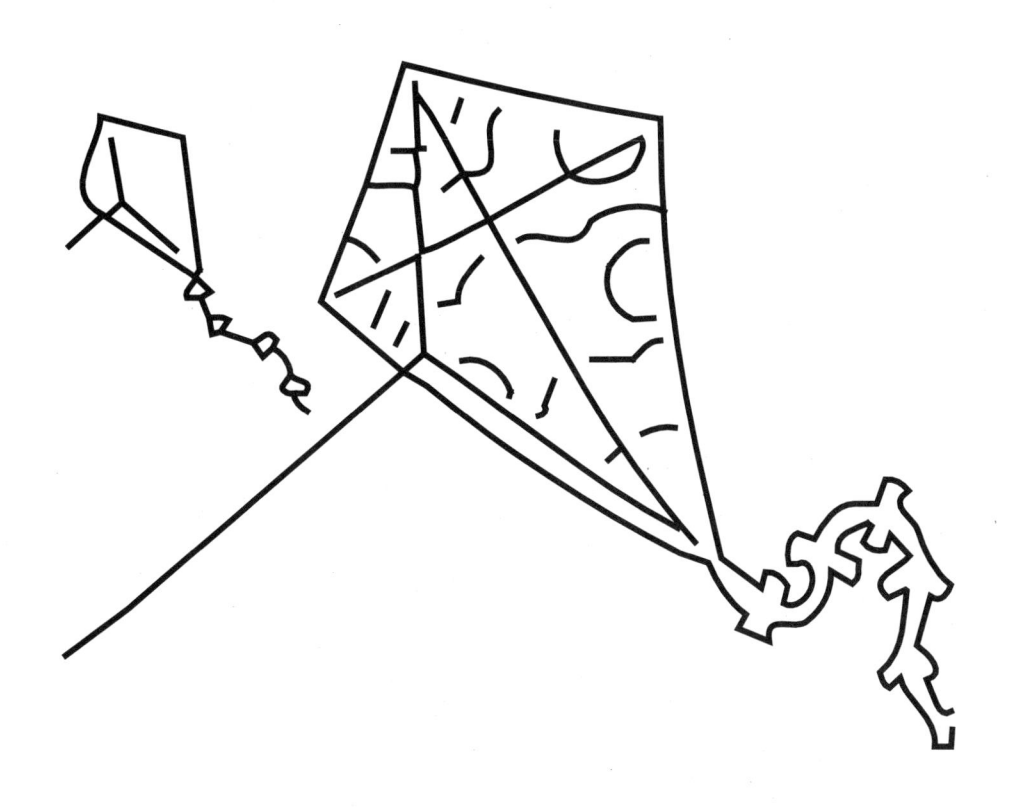

Blackline Master **46A-2**

© NTC / Contemporary Publishing Group

Español para ti Level Three

Blackline Master **46A-3**

© NTC / Contemporary Publishing Group

Español para ti Level Three

Blackline Master **46B-1**

© NTC / Contemporary Publishing Group

Español para ti Level Three

Blackline Master **46B-2**

© NTC / Contemporary Publishing Group

Español para ti Level Three

Blackline Master **46B-3**

Español para ti Level Three

Blackline Master **47A-1**

© NTC / Contemporary Publishing Group

Español para ti Level Three

Blackline Master **47A-2**

© NTC / Contemporary Publishing Group

Español para ti Level Three

Blackline Master **47A-3**

© NTC / Contemporary Publishing Group

Español para ti Level Three

Blackline Master **47A-4**

© NTC / Contemporary Publishing Group

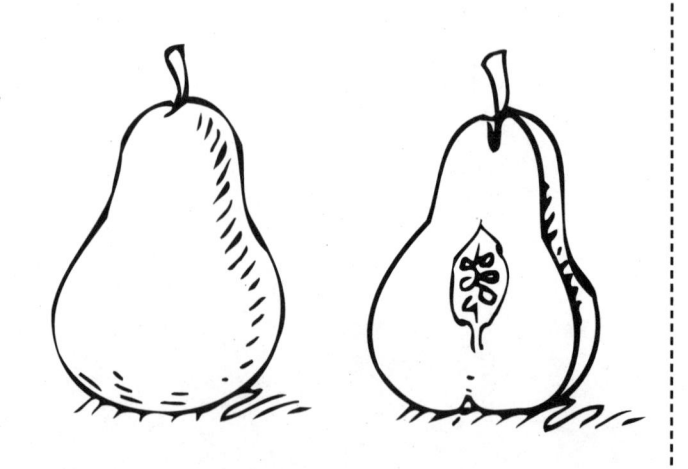

Español para ti Level Three

Blackline Master **51B**

© NTC / Contemporary Publishing Group

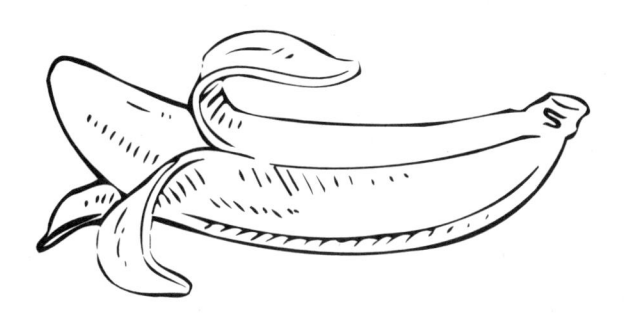

Español para ti Level Three

Blackline Master **52A**

© NTC / Contemporary Publishing Group

Español para ti Level Three

Blackline Master **52B**

Me gusta

Me gustan

© NTC / Contemporary Publishing Group

Español para ti Level Three

Blackline Master **53B**

uvas
piña
pera
manzana
limón
plátano
naranja
fresas

© NTC / Contemporary Publishing Group

Español para ti Level Three

Blackline Master **54A**

Me gusta

Me gustan

1) 
2) 
3) 
4) 
5) 
6) 
7)
8)

© NTC / Contemporary Publishing Group

Español para ti — Level Three

Blackline Master **55A**

© NTC / Contemporary Publishing Group

Español para ti Level Three

Blackline Master **56C**

1. gato

2. Jorge

3. Mano Mágica

4. amigos

5. me gusta

© NTC / Contemporary Publishing Group

Español para ti Level Three

Blackline Master **57A**

© NTC / Contemporary Publishing Group

La manzana se pasea.

De la sala al comedor.

No la comas con cuchara.

Cómela con tenedor.

1. silla

2. servilleta

3. cuchillo

4. llueve

5. sillón

1. vaca

2. verano

3. televisión

4. vocales

5. vuelta